SCORING RUBRICS IN THE CLASSROOM

EXPERTS IN ASSESSMENT™

SERIES EDITORS
THOMAS R. GUSKEY AND ROBERT J. MARZANO

JUDITH ARTER, JAY MCTIGHE
SCORING RUBRICS IN THE CLASSROOM: USING PERFORMANCE CRITERIA FOR
ASSESSING AND IMPROVING STUDENT PERFORMANCE

JANE M. BAILEY, THOMAS R. GUSKEY
IMPLEMENTING STUDENT-LED CONFERENCES

GREGORY J. CIZEK
DETECTING AND PREVENTING CLASSROOM CHEATING

LORNA M. EARL
ASSESSMENT AS LEARNING: USING CLASSROOM ASSESSMENT TO MAXIMIZE
STUDENT LEARNING

THOMAS R. GUSKEY, JANE M. BAILEY
DEVELOPING GRADING AND REPORTING SYSTEMS FOR STUDENT LEARNING

EDWARD KIFER
LARGE-SCALE ASSESSMENT: DIMENSIONS, DILEMMAS, AND POLICY

ROBERT J. MARZANO
DESIGNING A NEW TAXONOMY OF EDUCATIONAL OBJECTIVES

JAMES H. MCMILLAN
ESSENTIAL ASSESSMENT CONCEPTS FOR TEACHERS AND ADMINISTRATORS

DOUGLAS B. REEVES
HOLISTIC ACCOUNTABILITY: SERVING STUDENTS, SCHOOLS, AND COMMUNITY

JEFFREY K. SMITH, LISA F. SMITH, RICHARD DE LISI
NATURAL CLASSROOM ASSESSMENT: DESIGNING SEAMLESS INSTRUCTION
AND ASSESSMENT

Please call our toll-free number (800–818–7243)
or visit our website (www.corwinpress.com)
to order individual titles or the entire series.

Scoring Rubrics in the Classroom

USING PERFORMANCE CRITERIA FOR ASSESSING
AND IMPROVING STUDENT PERFORMANCE

Judith Arter

NORTHWEST REGIONAL EDUCATIONAL LABORATORY

Jay McTighe

Experts in Assessment™

SERIES EDITORS
THOMAS R. GUSKEY AND ROBERT J. MARZANO

CORWIN PRESS, INC.
A Sage Publications Company
Thousand Oaks, California

For information:

Corwin Press, Inc.
A Sage Publications Company
2455 Teller Road
Thousand Oaks, California 91320
E-mail: order@corwinpress.com

Sage Publications Ltd.
6 Bonhill Street
London EC2A 4PU
United Kingdom

Sage Publications India Pvt. Ltd.
M-32 Market
Greater Kailash I
New Delhi 110 048 India

Printed in the United States of America

Library of Congress Cataloging-in-Publication Data

Arter, Judith A.
    Scoring rubrics in the classroom: Using performance criteria for assessing and improving student performance / by Judith Arter and Jay McTighe.
      p. cm.—(Experts in assessment kit)
    Includes bibliographical references and index.
    ISBN 0-7619-7574-8 (cloth: alk. paper)
    ISBN 0-7619-7575-6 (pbk.: alk. paper)
    1. Competency-based educational tests—United States. 2. Grading and marking (Students)—United States. I. McTighe, Jay. II. Title. III. Series
    LC1034 .A78 2000
    371.27'0973—dc21   00-009504

This book is printed on acid-free paper.

06 7

Corwin Editorial Assistant: Catherine Kantor
Production Editor: Denise Santoyo
Editorial Assistant: Candice Crosetti
Copy Editor: Joyce Kuhn
Typesetter: Lynn Miyata
Cover Designer: Tracy E. Miller

Contents

Series Editors' Introduction   vii

Preface   ix

Book Content   xii

About the Authors   xv

1. Mapping the Terrain   1

What are performance criteria and rubrics, and how can they support instruction and improve student achievement?

Big Picture, Part 1: Balanced Assessment and the
Need for Performance Criteria   2

Big Picture, Part 2: The Definition of Performance Criteria   3

Big Picture, Part 3: The Kind of Criteria Covered in This Book
and the Kind Not Covered   4

Benefits of Performance Criteria for Teachers   8

Benefits of Performance Criteria for Students   12

Big Picture, Part 4: Performance Criteria and
Standards-Based Education   15

Chapter Summary   16

2. Choices, Choices, Choices   17

What types of rubrics exist, and how are they best used?

Choice #1: Holistic or Analytical Trait Rubrics?   18

Choice #2: Generic (General) or Task-Specific Rubrics?   24

Choice #3: Number of Score Points   29

Chapter Summary   32

3. Developing Rubrics   33

How do we design effective scoring rubrics?

Getting Started   33

Examples of Rubric Development   36

Chapter Summary   44

4. A Rubric for Rubrics: or, It's Metarubric Time   **45**

   How will we know when we have an effective rubric?

   A Rubric for Rubrics   45

   Metarubric Trait 1: Content/Coverage   53

   Metarubric Trait 2: Clarity/Detail   60

   Metarubric Trait 3: Usability   66

   Metarubric Trait 4: Technical Quality   69

   Chapter Summary   71

5. Performance Standards and Grading   **73**

   How good is good enough?

   Setting Performance Standards   74

   Grading   77

   Bottom Line on Grading   80

   Chapter Summary   81

6. Teaching Performance Criteria to Students   **82**

   How can we use rubrics to improve, as well as judge,
   student performance?

   Strategy 1: Teach Students the Language They Need
     to Think and Speak Like Writers   85

   Strategy 2: Read and Score Anonymous Student Papers   88

   Strategy 3: Practice-Focused Revision   88

   Strategy 4: Read, Read, READ!   90

   Strategy 5: Model the Writing Process Yourself   91

   Strategy 6: Give Students Many Opportunities to
     Show What They Know   92

   Strategy 7: Teach Lessons Focused on the Traits   93

   Chapter Summary   93

   Final Thoughts   94

Resource: Rubrics Galore   **95**

Glossary   **179**

References and Further Readings   **183**

Index   **185**

Series Editors' Introduction

Standards, assessment, accountability, and grading—these are the issues that dominated discussions of education in the 1990s. Today, they are at the center of every modern education reform effort. As educators turn to the task of implementing these reforms, they face a complex array of questions and concerns that little in their background or previous experience has prepared them to address. This series is designed to help in that challenging task.

In selecting the authors, we went to individuals recognized as true experts in the field. The ideas of these scholar-practitioners have already helped shape current discussions of standards, assessment, accountability, and grading. But equally important, their work reflects a deep understanding of the complexities involved in implementation. As they developed their books for this series, we asked them to extend their thinking, to push the edge, and to present new perspectives on what should be done and how to do it. That is precisely what they did. The books they crafted provide not only cutting edge perspectives but also practical guidelines for successful implementation.

We have several goals for this series. First, that it be used by teachers, school leaders, policy makers, government officials, and all those concerned with these crucial aspects of education reform. Second, that it helps broaden understanding of the complex issues involved in standards, assessment, accountability, and grading. Third, that it leads to more thoughtful policies and programs. Fourth, and most important, that it helps accomplish the basic goal for which all reform initiatives are intended—namely, to enable all students to learn excellently and to gain the many positive benefits of that success.

— *Thomas R. Guskey*
— *Robert J. Marzano*
Series Editors

Preface

Have you ever been nervous about grading certain types of student work—like creative writing, a research report, or an oral presentation? Have you ever been anxious because your new state content standards said that students "will think critically" or will be "life-long learners" and you are not quite sure how to ensure that they become so or even if you'll know when it occurs? Have you ever given up on peer-review groups because it seems to be a waste of time—students make very superficial comments to each other and you're not sure what to do about it? Have you ever pulled your hair out at 11:00 at night because it's obvious in the papers you're grading that your students just don't get it?

If so, then this book is for you. It is intended as a practical guide to the development and use of scoring rubrics in the classroom to achieve three goals:

1. Clarifying the targets of instruction, especially those that are complex and hard to define such as problem solving, writing, and group process skills

2. Providing valid and reliable assessment of student learning on these same complex and hard-to-assess student outcomes

3. Improving student motivation and achievement by helping students understand the nature of quality for performances and products

Consider the four vignettes in Box P.1 with these benefits in mind. Which scenarios will most likely lead to (a) reduced teacher anxiety about consistent and effective scoring of performance and (b) increased student confidence and achievement? Why?

> **BOX P.1   Vignettes**
>
> **Vignette 1: High School Science**
>
> Two years ago, the five teachers in a high school science department
> worked together to develop a common scoring rubric for a labora-
> tory report. They pooled their collective wisdom and looked at actual
> samples of student lab reports. Over time, their thinking led them to a consider-
> ation of the role of lab reports in promoting the larger goals of student reasoning,
> science process skills, and communicating effectively in science. Eventually, these
> features appeared in the rubric as a way to track the development of these compe-
> tencies in the context of lab reports. During the first week of each semester, the
> teachers distribute the rubric and review the criteria with the students to ensure that
> they clearly understand the important elements of a quality report and how their re-
> ports will be evaluated. Sample reports illustrating strong and weak performance on
> the criteria are discussed. The teachers have observed that the overall quality of stu-
> dent lab reports has improved since they all began using the same rubric consis-
> tently within the department.
>
>
>
> **Vignette 2: Sixth-Grade Mathematics**
>
> The following problem was presented to elementary children: "Three
> buses arrive in camp at 6:00 a.m. The first bus had 6 children, the
> second bus had 8 children, and the third bus had 7 children. How
> many children arrived at camp at 6:00 a.m.?" One student answered 21 kids. The
> teacher marked it wrong. He asked his mother why, and his mother told him to ask
> his teacher because she thought it was correct. When the student asked his teacher,
> she said, "Because you said 'kids' instead of 'children.'"
>
> **Vignette 3: Fourth-Grade Oral Presentation**
>
> A fourth-grade teacher introduced her students to the qualities of an
> effective oral presentation by showing them videotaped examples of
> excellent, as well as poor, speeches and presentations. Guided by
> the teacher, the students identified four key criteria (traits) that they
> agreed were important for an effective speech—content, organization, delivery, and
> language. They defined each of these and decided what would constitute strong,
> middle, and weak performance on each trait. They then referred to these perfor-
> mance criteria when preparing for their own speeches, and the teacher used the
> same criteria when providing feedback on, and grading, their presentations.

(continued)

> **BOX P.1** continued
>
>
>
> ### Vignette 4: Middle-School Social Studies
>
> A middle school student spent many hours working on her social studies "museum display" on the Gold Rush. She received a "B" on her project with no other comments. Being a high achiever, she expressed concern that she had met the project guidelines and asked the teacher what she could have done to get an "A." The teacher responded, "I reserve 'A' for a highly creative project." When asked for an example, the teacher replied, "Well, you could have presented it from the point of view of the Native Americans affected by the Gold Rush."

Vignettes 1 and 3

You, like most other teachers, undoubtedly identified Vignettes 1 and 3 as having the most positive benefits for teachers and students because they reveal three important principles regarding the effective use of performance criteria and scoring rubrics for evaluating and improving the quality of student performance.

1. Mutual agreement on the important qualities of student products (e.g., lab report) and performances (e.g., oral presentation) enables **more consistent evaluation** since the performance criteria do not vary from teacher to teacher. This increases teacher and student confidence.

2. When performance criteria are made public, there is **no "mystery"** as to the desired elements of quality or the basis for judging (and grading) student products and performances. Good-quality criteria provide clear instructional targets for teachers and learning targets for students. This also increases teacher and student confidence.

3. **Involving students** in generating and using criteria for self- and peer assessment helps them "get their minds around" important elements of quality and use that knowledge **to improve their own performance.** This increases student motivation, confidence, and achievement.

You probably also identified Vignettes 2 and 4 as being much less conducive to teacher and student confidence and achievement.

Vignette 2

In the second vignette, the teacher has focused on the use of correct units as the major criterion for performance. Now, we'll agree that units of measurement are important, although we might quibble whether a "kid" and a "child" are different units of measurement. But, if it is going to count, students need to know it. This child had enough gumption to ask "Why?" But what about another student who doesn't? Maybe next time he'll say to himself, "I think I got it right, but then I thought I got it right last time. Maybe I just don't understand."

The point? If we want students to take control of their own learning, they must know the criteria for quality. Without this knowledge, the student is left to guess what the teacher is after and will be unable to accurately self-assess and adjust. Additionally, these experiences can breed a feeling of hopelessness in students, resulting in their giving up.

(Additionally, the criteria have to be good. Is the distinction between "kid" and "child" an important distinction for a quality response? This makes one wonder whether the teacher really thought through the scoring guide she was using.)

Vignette 4

The example of the "Gold Rush museum display" renders school a "mystery game," where the student is left to guess what the teacher wants. The feedback system in this vignette (a single letter grade) provides no meaningful information about what the student has done well or any guidance about how she could improve.

The ensuing discussion with the teacher would undoubtedly breed frustration—if "creativity" were important, then why wasn't that made clear in advance? Additionally, what does "creativity" mean? The teacher might feel less than satisfied with her own ability to judge creativity, thus increasing the teacher's anxiety. The student is also left confused about what it takes to succeed, thus once again sapping her ability to self-assess and probably also decreasing her motivation to want to try in the future.

Book Content

These vignettes provide windows into the major themes in this book: how to use clearly stated performance criteria and scoring rubrics to make fair and consistent judgments about student performance, and how to use performance criteria and rubrics as tools to improve the very achievement that is being assessed.

. Each chapter is framed by a guiding question, includes illustrative stories, provides practical examples, offers tips and cautions, and concludes with a summary of key points.

Chapter 1 provides a "map of the terrain." We present definitions for key terms, provide the context for thinking about performance assessment and rubrics, and expand on the benefits to teachers and students of using rubrics. *Guiding Question: What are performance criteria and rubrics, and how can they support instruction and improve student achievement?*

In Chapter 2, we examine different types of scoring rubrics—holistic, analytic trait, generic, and task specific and discuss the appropriate uses, strengths, and limitations of each. *Guiding Question: What types of rubrics exist, and how are they best used?*

Chapter 3 describes a process for designing scoring rubrics. We present principles of effective rubric design and consider design options—traits, score scale, and descriptive language for distinguishing performance levels. *Guiding Question: How do we design effective scoring rubrics?*

In Chapter 4, we "walk the talk" by describing the qualities of an effective rubric. We examine both strong rubrics and common flaws in rubrics that illustrate the use of a "rubric for rubrics" to evaluate and improve rubric designs. *Guiding Question: How will we know when we have an effective rubric?*

In Chapter 5, we present options for establishing performance standards. We describe a process for selecting "anchors" to illustrate the various levels of quality described in the performance scale, and examine the relationship of rubric scores and letter grades. *Guiding Question: How good is "good enough"?*

In Chapter 6, we link assessment and instruction by exploring the use of rubrics as instructional tools to involve students in their own assessment and improve student performance. Practical strategies for teaching performance criteria to students, involving students in peer and self-assessment, providing student-friendly feedback, and the instructional use of anchors are offered. *Guiding Question: How can we use rubrics to improve, as well as judge, student performance?*

The book contains a glossary of key terms, a combined reference and further readings list (by chapter), and a "sampler" (in the Resource section) containing numerous examples of scoring rubrics for various grade levels and subject/performance areas.

Note: The Northwest Regional Educational Laboratory owns the following Trademarks, which are acknowledged throughout this book.
- Six-Trait Writing™
- 6 + 1 Traits™
- Traits of an Effective Reader™
- Mathematics Problem-Solving Model™
- Science Inquiry Model™

About the Authors

Judith A. Arter is a nationally recognized expert who has worked in the area of performing assessment for the past 21 years. She has codirected statewide writing assessments, developed classroom-based assessments for competency assessment, helped develop district performance assessments (mathematics, fine arts, foreign language, physical education, writing), developed training videos, reviewed hundreds of assessments from around the world, and is involved with many ongoing professional development activities. She directed Northwest Regional Educational Laboratory's assessment unit, which includes both a lending library of assessment tools and initiatives in portfolios, classroom assessment, writing assessment, reading assessment, oral communication assessment, self-study kits, and using assessment as tools for instruction in the classroom. She currently is National Training Director for the Assessment Training Institute in Portland, Oregon. Her background is in mathematics, special education, assessment, and Title I. She spent two years as district office staff member in Arizona and 21 years at NWREL. She has held teaching certificates in both elementary education and special education.

Jay McTighe served as Director of the Maryland Assessment Consortium, a state collaboration of school districts working together to develop and share formative performance assessments. Prior to this position, he was involved with school improvement projects at Maryland State Department of Education. He is well known for his work in "thinking skills," having coordinated statewide efforts to develop instructional strategies, curriculum models, and assessment procedures for improving the quality of student thinking. He also directed the development of the Instructional Framework, a multimedia database on teaching. In addition to his work at the state level, he has experience at the district level in Prince George's County, Maryland, as a classroom teacher, resource specialist, and program coordinator. He also served as director of the Maryland Summer Center for Gifted and Talented Students, a statewide residential enrichment program held at St. Mary's College. He has published articles in a number of leading journals and books, including *Educational Leadership* (ASCD), *Developing Minds* (ASCD), *Thinking Skills: Concepts and Techniques* (NEA), and *The Developer* (National Staff Development Council). He coauthored two books on assessment: *Assessing Outcomes: Performance Assessment Using the Dimensions of Learning Model* and *Assessing Learning in* *the Classroom.* He is coauthor, with Grant Wiggins, of two recently released books: *Understanding by Design* and *Understanding by Design Handbook.* He has an extensive background in staff development and is a regular speaker at national, state, and district conferences and workshops. He is also a featured presenter in two videotapes: *Performance Assessment in the Classroom* from the Video Journal of Education and *Developing Performance Assessments* from ASCD. He received his undergraduate degree from the College of William and Mary, earned a master's degree from the University of Maryland, and has completed postgraduate studies at Johns Hopkins University. He was selected to participate in the Educational Policy Fellowship Program through the Institute for Educational Leadership in Washington, D.C. He served as a member of the National Assessment Forum, a coalition of education and civil rights organizations advocating reforms in national, state, and local assessment policies and practices. He also completed a three-year term on the ASCD Publications Committee, serving as committee chair during 1994-1995.

CHAPTER 1

Mapping the Terrain

Guiding Question: *What are performance criteria and rubrics, and how can they support instruction and improve student achievement?*

Recently, I (Judith Arter) visited a school that was using a rubric for good quality writing to teach and assess writing (in this case, the Six-Trait Model, which is included in the Resource section). The teachers, students, and parents loved the process because they could clearly see what it took to succeed. It also enabled teachers to focus instruction and reliably track student progress over time. Students amazed everyone by their ability to accurately self-assess and self-correct. Writing achievement was steadily improving.

During the course of conversation about their successful project I asked the principal, "Isn't this a great example of standards-based instruction?" I wasn't grilling the principal, I was just excited about how their activities exemplified the best intentions of standards-based learning.

The principal's reply brought me up short. She said, "What do you mean? We're just using the Six-Trait Model to teach and assess writing."

It became very apparent that, although this staff was successfully using a rubric to focus teaching and help students improve their writing performance, they may not have completely understood how their practice fits into the bigger picture of assessment and standards-based education. As a result, they may not have been able to fully justify nor explain to others what they were doing. Similarly, they may not have been fully able to generalize the use of rubrics to other content areas.

So, we're going to begin by providing the "bigger picture" of the use of assessment, performance criteria, and scoring rubrics in standards-based education. We'll consider four bits of contextual information: how rubrics and performance assessment fit into classroom assessment in general, what rubrics are, what we are and aren't going to cover in this book, and standards-

1

based education. Along the way we'll expand on the benefits of performance criteria and rubrics for teachers and students.

Big Picture, Part 1: Balanced Assessment and the Need for Performance Criteria

The first bit of needed context answers the question "What are performance criteria, and how do they fit into the total picture of classroom assessment?"

What assessment methods do you use in the classroom? Multiple-choice? Matching? True/False? Essay? Performance assessment? Conferencing? Observation? While a variety of assessment methods are available, they fall into two broad categories: (1) selected-response/short-answer and (2) constructed-response.

We're throwing these terms at you because they bear directly on the need for performance criteria—selected-response questions don't need performance criteria, but *all* constructed-response methods do.

Selected-response (multiple choice, true-false, and matching) and **short-answer** methods require that students select a response from a provided list or require that students supply a very brief answer. These formats are great and very useful! You can use them to efficiently assess students' knowledge of factual information, basic concepts, and simple skills. Since such assessment items typically have a correct or best response, student answers may be quickly and "objectively" scored as correct or incorrect (but see Box 1.1). The term "objective test items" is sometimes used to describe selected-response assessment methods because the answers are "objectively" scored—they are either right or wrong; there is no middle ground.

Despite these advantages, we all know the limitations of selected-response and short-answer items. First, an important goal for students is to be able to apply knowledge and reasoning in meaningful, "real world" situations. Selected-response questions tend to assess knowledge and skills in isolated, decontextualized ways. If we want application to the real world, we need another assessment technique.

Second, there is no hope of even assessing certain kinds of important student learning outcomes in selected-response and short-answer formats. Consider writing, oral communication, physical skills, reading rate, and so on.

> **BOX 1.1**　Misconception Alert!
>
> There is actually nothing "objective" about selected-response test questions except the scoring. Subjective judgments enter all the way through the development of selected-response questions— What content should be covered? What specific questions should be asked? How should these questions be worded? What incorrect choices should be included? So, the idea that somehow selected-response questions are more "objective" than constructed-response questions is a common misconception.

For these types of outcomes, **constructed-response** assessments are the ticket. Constructed-response assessments include essay tests, which ask students to prepare a lengthy written response to a question. Constructed-response assessments also include performance assessments where students construct a tangible product (written, visual, or three-dimensional) or perform a demonstration (drive, speak, work in a group, play an instrument) to show what they understand and can do. Since constructed-response assessments call for students to organize and use knowledge and skills to answer a question or complete a task, rather than to recall and recognize, they are more likely to reveal if students understand and can apply what they're learning.

Now here's the fly in the constructed-response ointment. Student responses to constructed-response assessments cannot be scored using a simple answer key or machine. As you know, a human being must rely on his or her own observation and judgment to evaluate responses to these open-ended assessments because they result in a range of responses that reveal different strategies, varying degrees of sophistication, and different levels of proficiency. Because of the need for humans to judge responses to constructed-response assessments, these formats have been labeled "subjective."

How are we going to reliably judge the quality of responses on constructed-response assessments? In other words, how can we even hope to make these "subjective" judgments as "objective" as possible? The answer is high-quality performance criteria that help us focus in on the most telling aspects of performance and be consistent with one another.

All constructed-response assessments require performance criteria.

> **BOX 1.2**
>
>
> *Which type of classroom assessment is best— selected- or constructed-response?* **Answer:** All of the above! We advocate a balanced assessment approach, whereby teachers regularly use a variety of assessment formats (selected-response, short-answer, essay, and performance assessments) matched to the desired achievement targets and assessment purposes.

Big Picture, Part 2:
The Definition of Performance Criteria

What do you think of when you hear the word "criteria"? Standards? Benchmarks? Features that distinguish quality? That which is valued? What to look for in work to grade it? Rubrics? Scoring guides?

Box 1.3 contains our definition for performance criteria. How does it match with yours?

> **BOX 1.3** Definition
>
> **Performance criteria** are guidelines, rules, or principles by which student responses, products, or performances are judged. They describe what to look for in student performances or products to judge quality.
>
>    Do you agree that whenever we make a judgment about anything we have criteria whether we can clearly articulate them or not?

What are your criteria for a quality restaurant? Tastiness of the food, ambience, cleanliness, price, service, convenience, . . . ? What are your criteria for a quality hotel? Décor, comfort, cost, amenities, location, . . . ? What are the criteria for excellence in Olympic diving? Form, splash, difficulty, . . . ?

The same question applies to areas of academic performance— what are the criteria for a quality oral presentation, science lab report, second-year foreign-language discussion, or cooperative group investigation?

If you're like most teachers, you observe students and make judgments about their work hundreds of times a day. Does Joe really understand this math concept? Is Jenelle's report worthy of an "A?" Did Juan understand what he just read? In each of these situations, criteria are used whether the teacher can articulate them or not.

Now, you might be saying "Whoa, that's just informal observation; it's not rigorous enough to be called 'performance assessment'." And you're right. Observation and judgment are essentially subjective. The goal with *any* constructed response and performance assessment—formal or informal—is to *make an essentially subjective process as clear, consistent, and defensible as possible. One does this through explicitly defined performance criteria.*

Big Picture, Part 3:
The Kind of Criteria Covered in This Book
and the Kind Not Covered

We can hear you begin to get nervous—"Are they really saying all open-ended questions I use in my classroom need performance criteria? Where will I get the time to develop and use them?"

The answer is "Well, yes," but they don't all need to be complicated. Some constructed-response questions only require simple criteria. For example, although reading rate requires a complex skill on the part of the student, the criterion for judging it is very simple—you come up with the number of words read per minute and compare it to a desirable rate at a particular grade or age.

_____	Date, flush left at top
_____	Address
_____	Greeting
_____	Body
_____	Salutation
_____	Signature

Figure 1.1. Checklist for a Friendly Letter

_____	Standing dribble with right hand—15 consecutive bounces
_____	Standing dribble with left hand—15 consecutive bounces
_____	Moving dribble (either hand)—5 consecutive bounces
_____	Free throw—5 made
_____	Lay up—5 made (either hand)
_____	Jump shot from outside the lane—3 made

Figure 1.2. Checklist for Basketball Skills

Scoring methods and performance criteria for constructed response and performance assessments are huge topics. So, we must narrow down what we discuss in this book. Specifically, we do *not* deal with simple criteria to assess simple things—checklists, or what we call "assessment lists." Rather, we place our emphasis on criteria for assessing more complicated things, which, for purposes of this book, we call "rubrics."

What We Do Not Cover in This Book

Checklists

You've all seen checklists. They list the components that must be present in a product or performance. You check off the ones that are present. Figures 1.1 and 1.2 present two examples of checklists.

Notice that *there is no judgment of quality in either example*. In the first, the six letter elements are either present or not. In the second, the skill is checked when the identified performance is attained.

Checklists are simple to use. But you can only use them where a judgment of "present or absent" is sufficient. Look at Box 1.4 for an example of what hap-

> **BOX 1.4**   Vignette: The Case of the Inadequate Checklist
>
> A fourth-grade teacher was trying to make sure that students included a beginning, middle, and end in their stories. She had a simple checklist that she shared with students—students checked off if they included a beginning, middle, and end. Then she began reading the papers. All the students had a beginning, middle, and end, *but some were better than others.* The teacher thought, "Is any beginning, middle, and end OK, or should I be teaching my students what constitutes a good beginning, middle, and end? Maybe this skill is more complicated than I thought."
>
>
> Then it came time for parent conferences. Parents had some questions about grades in writing—why did all students get the same grade when their writing varied so obviously in quality?
>
> What should the teacher do? The teacher needs more sophisticated criteria for writing—ones that really do enable students, parents, and teachers to discern levels of quality.

pened when a teacher tried to use a checklist when a more sophisticated scoring method was necessary.

Because checklists do not provide detailed descriptions of levels of quality, they are not appropriate to use in assessing performances having a fuller range of qualitatively different performance levels. While we, the authors, think that checklists are wonderful, practical tools for certain situations, we won't deal with how to develop or use checklists in this book. Our focus is on more sophisticated scoring systems.

Performance Lists

A more sophisticated scoring tool than checklists consists of a list of things to rate and a rating scale. Two examples of criterion-based performance lists are provided in Figures 1.3 and 1.4.

The performance list for a graph (Figure 1.3) contains seven criterion elements. Each element is "scored" based upon the possible number of points listed. An overall score of 30 points is possible.

Figure 1.4 presents an example of a performance list for use in the primary grades. In this case, students' pictures are judged against a 3-point scale (Terrific, Good, Needs Work).

Both examples reveal the strengths and limitations of this type of scoring tool. On the plus side, performance lists offer more score choices than checklists—up to five points in the first example and three choices in the second.

Element	Points Possible	Points Earned Self	Points Earned Teacher
1. An appropriate type of graph is used.	5		
2. An appropriate title is given.	3		
3. Horizontal and vertical axes are drawn and labeled correctly.	4		
4. Intervals on the axes are labeled and spaced appropriately.	4		
5. A key for both sets of data is shown.	4		
6. Both sets of data are plotted accurately on the graph.	6		
7. The graph is neat and easy to interpret.	4		

Figure 1.3. Performance List for a Graph

SOURCE: From *Performance Assessment Tasks, V. 9.* © Maryland Assessment Consortium. Used with permission.

My picture shows how a flood affects people and plants.

My sentence(s) have correct information about a flood.

My picture shows how a drought affects people and plants.

My sentence(s) have correct information about a drought.

Figure 1.4. Performance List for Picture: Comparison of Floods/Drought

SOURCE: From *Performance Assessment Tasks: Primary Level, V. 8.* © Maryland Assessment Consortium. Used with permission.

They also give you the flexibility to weigh certain elements over others (e.g., accuracy counts more than neatness).

Despite these benefits, performance lists reveal a major weakness—a lack of detailed description of the performance levels. For example, in Figure 1.3, what exactly is the difference between a "2" and a "5" for "an appropriate type of graph"? Despite identified criteria, judgments remain fairly subjective. In fact, different teachers using the same performance list may rate the same student's work quite differently. In the absence of detailed descriptions of performance levels, teachers' differing expectations and performance standards make reliable evaluation a challenge.

Again, we're not rejecting the use of performance lists. They can be perfectly adequate for judging certain simple products or performances. Nonetheless, we do not focus on this type of scoring tool.

BOX 1.5 Definition
A **rubric** is a particular format for criteria—it is the written-down version of the criteria, with all score points described and defined. The best rubrics are worded in a way that covers the essence of what we, as teachers, look for when we're judging quality, and they reflect the best thinking in the field as to what constitutes good performance. Rubrics are frequently accompanied by examples (anchors) of products or performances to illustrate the various score points on the scale.

What We *Do* Focus On: Rubrics!

This book concentrates on **rubrics**—scoring tools containing criteria and a performance scale that allows us to define and describe the most important components that comprise *complex* performances and products. Our definition is given in Box 1.5. An example of a rubric is shown in Figure 1.5.

Notice that the rubric provides a description of the levels of performance, unlike a performance list, which simply assigns scores based on identified criterion elements.

Benefits of Performance Criteria for Teachers

We've alluded to benefits before, but now we're going to be specific. We have observed two primary benefits of performance criteria and scoring guides for teachers.

Benefit 1: Consistency in Scoring

Let's return to the first question posed in this book: Have you ever been nervous grading student essays, responses to

High—The student

➤ Initiates identifying needed group roles and accepts responsibility for fulfilling an assigned role

➤ Invites contributions from others

➤ Acknowledges the statements of others in a way that builds a consecutive interchange between participants

➤ When disagreeing, does so respectfully

➤ Makes sure that all relevant points of view are heard

➤ Is aware of cultural differences in social interactions and behaves in an appropriate fashion

➤ Attempts to resolve conflicts when they arise

➤ Shares decision making

Middle—The student

➤ Participates in the development of the group process when initiated by others

➤ Attends to the discussion but doesn't participate very much

➤ Responds to the solicitation of opinions or ideas but doesn't volunteer them

➤ Does not detract from the functioning of the group

Low—The student

➤ Does not fulfill assigned roles

➤ Makes irrelevant or distracting statements

➤ Monopolizes the conversation

➤ Makes a personal attack

➤ Is uninvolved in the discussion, even when directly asked for an opinion

Figure 1.5. Rubric for Group Interaction

open-ended mathematics problems, research reports, or other complex performances and products? If you are like most educators, the answer is "Yes." Why is this? Doubts like these run through our minds: "Maybe I'm not really noticing the most important dimensions of performance." "Maybe I'm not being consistent between students." "Maybe Mrs. Jones next door wouldn't agree with my grades."

Clearly defined performance criteria communicate the important dimensions, or elements of quality, in a product or performance. The clarity provided by well-defined criteria assists us in reducing subjective judgments when evaluating student work. When a common set of performance criteria and scoring guides are used throughout a department or grade-level team, school, or district, this benefit is extended, increasing the consistency of judgments across teachers.

Have you had this experience?

Benefit 2: Improved Instruction

A second benefit of explicitly developed performance criteria relates to teaching. Clearly defined criteria and scoring guides provide more than just evaluation tools to use at the end of instruction—they help clarify instructional goals and serve as teaching targets.

Educators who have scored student work as part of a large-scale performance assessment at the district or state level often recognize this benefit. For example, educators using the Six-Trait Model for evaluating writing unanimously agree that the very process of assessing teaches a great deal about what makes writing successful. Raters have to internalize a set of criteria so thoroughly that they can be consistent both with themselves, over time, and with other raters. During the process of scoring hundreds of papers, raters see many examples of what good and poor writing looks like, and they learn to systematically analyze it to determine why it is good or poor. Stories from raters (see Box 1.6) indicate that, for many, this assessment experience marks the first time they truly feel confident that they can identify the features of effective writing, in large part because they have a systematic vocabulary for talking about these features. Teachers go back to the classroom much more confident about their day-to-day judgments of student work and their ability to teach students how to craft writing so that it is effective.

Have you also noticed this?

What are our criteria for quality critical thinking, life-long learning, perseverance, motivation to learn, science progress skills, or math problem solving? If you are like most other educators, your notion of what constitutes good quality in these areas is not as crystal clear as your notion of what you like in a restaurant or other things in daily life. And yet, as educators, we are being asked to ensure that students are critical thinkers, life-long learners, and so on. How can we do this if it is not clear to us what it looks like when students are doing these things well? *And, it is the most complex skills that most need this definition.*

Good quality performance criteria help teachers answer questions like these:

> **BOX 1.6** Quotes and References:
> Importance of Criteria for Teachers
>
> "In my work with teachers, it is the skill of 'rubric writing' which is most elusive. Perhaps it's because we're used to assigning single grades for complex assignments, knowing what an 'A' looks like in our heads, but rarely 'putting it to paper' so that our students can see it as well. Perhaps the difficulty in writing scoring criteria also lies in the challenge of describing just what it really looks like to perform well, or better yet, to perform at a variety of levels of competency. Nevertheless, it is the use of rubrics as an indispensable part of the instructional process which completes the vital link between assessment and instruction. Until we invest the time discerning for ourselves what excellence in writing, or speaking, or dancing, or singing, or whatever looks like, we are unable to fully 'teach' our students to achieve at these levels."
>
> —*Scott Mendel, on creating portraits of performance, Peakview Elementary School, 19451 East Progress Circle, Aurora, CO 90015*
>
>
> "I'm going to be very honest. When I went to high school and college, English composition was not my favorite subject. I never had success in it. I always knew on my papers what I did wrong, but I didn't know what to do to fix them. All of a sudden I'm into the classroom. . . . All the subjects were easy . . . except composition. I was a little bit nervous about how to grade them. I never really knew what to look for. . . . But, that's all changed. By writing with my students, and by going through the process with them [using the Six-Trait Model for writing], I've learned success right along with my kids."
>
> —*Rhonda Woodruff, Beaverton School District, Oregon, discussing her use of the Six-Traits + 1 Model to teach students to self-assess and improve their own writing.*

- What is expected?
- What are our standards?
- What does good performance look like?
- What do I want to accomplish?
- What kind of feedback do I give to improve student work next time?
- Where are my students on their journey to competence, and what is the next step in instruction?
- Is my instruction effective?

The vocabulary for describing quality work, and the practice of systematically applying quality criteria to lots of student work, has the potential of turning subjective, informal teacher classroom observation into objective, trusted observations on student progress and status. Although it might require a lot of work at the outset, good quality, internalized performance criteria are, in the long run, a great time-saver.

Benefits of Performance Criteria for Students

If the use of well-defined performance criteria brings about a shared vocabulary and a clearer understanding of the important dimensions of quality performance for educators, then couldn't students also realize similar benefits? The answer is YES!

To explore this idea, consider the true story in Box 1.7 about criteria for passing the driver's test in Washington State.

What percentage of student drivers in Washington State do you think actually know on what basis their driving performance will be evaluated? Do you believe that it is important for examinees to know the criteria on which they'll be judged? Of course, we're counting on your response to be a resounding "YES!"

If we want to provide clear learning goals for students and remove the "mystery" of what it takes to succeed, it is essential that students know the performance criteria. Knowledge of criteria enables students to focus in practice and feel more in control. As assessment expert Richard Stiggins (2001) notes, "Students can hit any target that they can clearly see and stands still for them."

When students know the criteria in advance of their performance, they are provided with clear goals for their work. They don't have to guess about what is most important or how their performance will be judged. When we share performance criteria and scoring guides with students, we offer them the opportunity to self-assess and improve their work along the way. Through this approach to the use of performance criteria and scoring guides, we can enhance the quality of student learning and performance, not simply evaluate it.

And, of course, this requires that the criteria are sound—they truly reflect the nature of quality in a product or performance. If the criteria leave important things out, include the trivial, or reward performance on features that do not really define quality, then students will learn according to the criteria presented, but they might not be hitting the desired target. For example, we recently saw a rubric for a poster. One of the listed criteria (needed to get a high score) specified that the poster "must have three colors." Our question is "Why?" What happens if a student develops a wonderful poster that gets its point across not through color but the lack of color? What's the target here—a colorful poster or an effective poster? Sometimes, color promotes effective-

> **BOX 1.7** Vignette: The Driver's Test
>
>
>
> As an example of performance assessment, talk in a workshop turned to the driver's test. As a result, one of the authors (Judy Arter) called up the DMV in Washington State to find out the criteria for passing the driver's test. What follows is the conversation with the DMV.
>
> *Judy:* "What are your criteria for the driver's test?"
>
> *Examiner:* "What do you mean?"
>
> *Judy:* "Well, you're sitting in the car watching the examinee drive and you have to make a decision as to whether the person will pass. On what basis do you make that decision?"
>
> *Examiner:* "I'll let you talk to my supervisor."
> Judy is put on hold. The supervisor answers.
>
> *Judy:* "What are your criteria for the driver's test?"
>
> *Supervisor:* "What do you mean?"
>
> *Judy:* "Well, is it a secret? Are we not supposed to know the basis on which we'll be judged?"
>
> *Supervisor:* "No, it's not that. I'm just curious as to why you want to know."
>
> *Judy* (after much explanation and further attempts, without success, to get the desired information): "Just tell me what's on the clipboard that the examiner has in the car."
>
> And here's what the supervisor said: Tasks for the driver's test in Washington State are stopping at stop signs, parking on a hill (very important in Washington State), backing around a corner, parallel parking, turning onto and off of one- and two-way streets, driving on freeways and surface streets, and so on. These probably look very similar to the tasks examinees have to perform in your state. Criteria for the driver's test in Washington State: The examiners look for control of the vehicle, obeying laws, looking (rearview mirror, over the shoulder—swivel head), and use of turn signals. But at the end of the test, all the observations are boiled down to judgments in three areas: (1) overall examinee skill level; (2) whether the examinee has caused congestion; and (3) whether the examinee has caused a danger.

ness, but sometimes it doesn't. Students need to know the difference between that which is *really* important and that which is merely a means to the end.

Is this instruction, or is it assessment? It's both—a perfect example of integrating assessment and instruction.

The importance of rubrics for helping students learn is well demonstrated by the quotes in Box 1.8.

BOX 1.8   Quotes and References:
Why Performance Criteria Are Important for Students

"Ultimately, we want students to grow to be independent. For them to do that, they have to have a sense of what the criteria are that make them successful. For a long time, the criteria have been a mystery to students."

—*Robert Tierney et al., "Portfolio Assessment in the*
Reading-Writing Classroom," NCTE, 1991.

"Scales, criteria, and specific questions which students apply to their own or others' writing also have a powerful effect on enhancing quality. Through using the criteria systematically, students appear to internalize them and bring them to bear in generating new material even when they do not have the criteria in front of them. These treatments are two times more effective than free writing techniques."

—*George Hillocks, "Research on Written Composition," NCTE, 1986.*

"While the purpose of student selection [in portfolios] is to engender and support a reflective and self-evaluative capacity, the developers recognized that this is possible only if students have deep understandings about the nature of quality in their work and are able to make judgments that accurately reflect a valid assessment of that quality."

—*Paul LeMahieu, Drew Gitomer, and JoAnne Eresh, "Portfolios in*
Large-Scale Assessment: Difficult But Not Impossible," Educational
Measurement: Issues and Practice, Fall, 1995, pp. 11–28.

"I purposefully came down to fourth grade to see if I could [teach writing using the Six-Trait Model rubric]. And you know what I found? Those younger students learn quicker. And I keep asking myself, why is it that young students can look at a piece of writing, look at their [rubric] guide, and be right on? I think it's because they don't have to reteach themselves. They don't have to erase something they've already learned that maybe didn't work so well."

—*Rhonda Woodruff, Beaverton School District, Oregon, on using the*
Six-Traits + 1 Model to teach writing to fourth graders.

And direct evidence of the impact of rubrics on student achievement is described in NSDC's journal *Results,* December/January 2000, pp. 1, 6:

Writing improvement is busting out all over. . . . At Aurora's (CO) Wheeling Elementary School, for example, the percentage of students writing at or above standard between 1997 and 1998 rose from 13% to 36%; at Leroy Drive Elementary in Adams County, from 13% to 45%; at Bessemer Elementary School in Pueblo—a school with an 8% minority population—from 2% to 48%. . . . Why are these schools experiencing such exceptional improvement in this area? George Hillocks . . . found that one of the most powerful interventions was using what he dubbed "scales"— his word for rubrics or scoring guides. Hillocks suggested that merely using a clear, common set of criteria guides teaching and accelerates learning.

Big Picture, Part 4: Performance Criteria and Standards-Based Education

We hear a lot these days about "standards-based education." There's an important connection between standards-based education and performance criteria.

Although the particulars may vary from place to place, standards-based education reflects the following fundamental characteristics:

- There are clearly stated long-term learning targets for students (content standards)—what we want students to know and be able to do when they complete their education.

- There are benchmarks along the way so that we know if students are on track.

- Instruction and assessment are aimed at these important targets and aligned across grade levels to reduce duplication and make it clear how the skills and understandings developed one year will be built upon the next.

- Standards-referenced descriptions of student learning are used rather than norm-referenced or self-referenced. Rather than comparing students to each other, we define the nature of quality (performance criteria) and set performance standards (how good is good enough) as a basis for judging student achievement and progress.

- The performance criteria and standards are made public so that everyone—students, teachers, parents, community members, and employers—are aware of the nature of excellence and what it takes to succeed. Students can see where they are, and teachers can tell parents how their children are progressing toward "proficiency."

Performance criteria and rubrics associated with constructed response and performance assessments serve important functions in such standards-based education:

- Performance criteria help define the standards by specifying what one would look for as evidence that the standards have been achieved. In fact, some folks think the criteria are the final definition of a standard—what is in the rubric is what teachers will teach and what students will learn.

- When made public, the performance criteria and scoring guides provide clear and consistent targets for students, parents, teachers, and others.

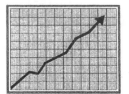

- When used consistently across classrooms, schools, and districts, the evaluation of student performance becomes more reliable.
- Teaching criteria to students helps improve the very skills being assessed, thus integrating assessment and instruction.

Chapter Summary

This chapter defined key vocabulary terms, described the role of performance criteria and rubrics in the bigger scheme of assessment and standards-based education, and presented the benefits of performance criteria for students and teachers.

BOX 1.9   Rubrics—In a Nutshell

Whenever you use constructed-response assessment questions, you need criteria. Some of these can be very simple, like checklists or "performance lists." Some of these need to be more complex in order to capture the nature of quality in the diversity of student work.

We use the term "rubric" for these more complex kinds of criteria. Good quality rubrics cover the essense of quality and carefully define levels of performance.

BOX 1.10   Benefits of Performance Criteria

1. To help educators clarify the nature of complex learning targets so that they feel comfortable teaching to them
2. To assess student progress and status in ways that are consistent across students, assignments, and time
3. To improve student achievement by letting students in on the secret of the nature of quality
4. Through all these things, to integrate assessment and instruction and grasp the essence of standards-based instruction

CHAPTER 2

Choices, Choices, Choices

Guiding Question: *What types of rubrics exist, and how are they best used?*

You say "holistic" and I say "analytical trait"—let's call the whole thing off! While it is true that there are some choices to be made with respect to rubrics, and these choices come equipped with odd terminology, the choices really arc relatively simple and logical.

Choices boil down to use. What is the job at hand? What arc you hoping a rubric will do for you? Is it to teach students the important aspects of a complex performance, or is it to get a quick overall estimate of group status? Is it to find out if students can apply a particular problem-solving strategy, or when given an open-ended problem, if they can bring whatever problem-solving resources to bear to come up with a good solution? Is it to certify student competence or enable students to track their own progress toward important learning outcomes?

All of these are legitimate uses of rubrics. Some types of rubrics are more efficient for certain uses than other types.

And that's what we discuss in this chapter—What types of rubrics exist? What are the distinguishing features of each? What are their strengths and weaknesses? When should the different types be used?

Just to keep the information straight, here's how the chapter is set up:

→ Each section outlines a choice to be made:

- Holistic or analytical trait

- Task specific or general

- Number of score points possible

→ For each choice, we include a picture (for those visual learners among us), a definition, examples, and guidance on use.

→ References from research or other articulate authors to show why we give the advice we do.

Our guidelines are only that—guidelines. These ideas are not engraved in stone and should not be taken to represent the truth in the universe. The goal is for the reader to become familiar enough with the possibilities that it becomes second nature to decide on a scoring mechanism for the products and performances that occur in the classroom. Use your own judgment! The important thing is to have good reasons why you choose what you do.

Choice #1: Holistic or Analytical Trait Rubrics?

A *holistic* rubric gives a single score or rating for an entire product or performance based on an overall impression of a student's work. In essence, one combines all the important ingredients of a performance or product to arrive at an overall, single judgment of quality. An example of a holistic rubric is shown in Figure 2.1.

Notice how the combining occurs in this example. To arrive at an overall quality judgment, the rater would consider mathematical understanding, problem solving sophistication, *and* quality of communication all together, mentally weigh them, and decide on a single score that best describes the overall performance.

An *analytical trait* rubric divides a product or performance into essential traits or dimensions so that they can be judged separately—one *analyzes* a product or performance for essential *traits*. A separate score is provided for each trait. An example of an analytical trait rubric is provided in Figure 2.2.

In this example, writing performance is examined on each of six traits: (1) ideas, (2) organization, (3) voice, (4) word choice, (5) sentence fluency, and (6) conventions. Different traits could get different scores. For example, a piece of writing might receive a "3" for ideas (trait #1), and a "5" for use of conventions (trait #6), and so on. This reveals a profile of strengths and weaknesses in a piece of work.

Just to be clear, there *are* holistic rubrics for writing. What's in them? The same dimensions and characteristics as those listed in Figure 2.2. The only difference is that instead of considering each trait separately, one combines all the traits together to come up with a single overall score.

Likewise, there *are* analytical trait rubrics for open-ended mathematics problems that parallel the holistic California example in Figure 2.1 (see Illinois Mathematics and NWREL Mathematics in the Resource section). What's in

Level 6: Solid work that may go beyond the requirements of the task(s), showing, for example,

> ➤ Complete understanding of the task's mathematical concepts and processes

> ➤ Clear identification of all of the important elements of the task(s)

> ➤ Where appropriate, clear evidence of doing purposeful mathematics . . .

> ➤ Excellent prose and mathematical supporting arguments that may include examples or counterexamples

> ➤ Unusual insights into the nature of the resolution of problems encountered in the task(s)

> ➤ . . .

Level 4: Substantially completes the requirements of the task(s), showing, for example,

> ➤ An understanding of most of the task's mathematical concepts and processes

> ➤ Identification of the important elements of the task(s), but some less important ideas are missing

> ➤ Some aspects of investigations . . . may be missing, but most of the parts are included

> ➤ Adequate communication with an identified audience, but with limited clarity and variety

> ➤ . . .

Level 1: Does not achieve any requirements of the task(s), showing, for example,

> ➤ An irrelevant, nonsensical, or illegible response that has no valid relationship to the task(s)

> ➤ No understanding of the task's mathematical concepts and processes

> ➤ An unsuccessful attempt, if any, to communicate with the intended audience . . .

> ➤ . . .

Figure 2.1. Holistic Rubric: California Mathematics

SOURCE: From *A Sampler of Mathematics Assessment—Addendum.* ©1994, California Department of Education. Used with permission.
Note: Only part of the rubric is presented here. See the Resource section for the complete rubric.

them? The same dimensions and characteristics as those listed in Figure 2.1. The only difference is that instead of combining all the features together, they are split up into logical groupings called traits. Each trait receives a separate score.

Each of the following traits—the important dimensions of a quality writing product—is scored separately on a 1–5 scale. Score points 5, 3, and 1 include descriptors. A score of 3 represents a balance of strengths and weaknesses; 2 demonstrates some characteristics of a 1 and some characteristics of a 3; 4 demonstrates some characteristics of a 5 and some characteristics of a 3.

Ideas: the heart of the message, the content of the piece, the main theme, together with the details that enrich and develop that theme

Organization: the internal structure of the writing, the thread of central meaning, the logical and sometimes intriguing pattern of the ideas

Voice: the feeling and/or conviction of the individual writing coming out through the words

Word Choice: rich, colorful, and/or precise language that moves and enlightens the reader

Sentence Fluency: the rhythm and flow of the language, the sound of word patterns, the way in which the writing plays to the ear—not just to the eye

Conventions: the mechanical correctness of the piece—spelling, grammar and usage, paragraphing, use of capitals, and punctuation

---

Figure 2.2. Analytical Trait Rubric: Six-Trait Writing
SOURCE: © 2000, NWREL. Portland, OR. Reprinted with permission.
Note: Only the trait definitions are included here. See the Resource section for the entire rubric.

How Many Slices (Traits)?

Any good rubric, holistic or analytical trait, will cover all the essential features of a performance—there are certain features of writing or mathematics problem solving or oral presentations that everyone agrees are important.

The only question is whether to leave the whole ball of wax as a ball (holistic scoring) or to group similar features together and slice the ball up into traits. The Six-Trait Model, for example slices the ball of quality writing features into six slices (traits). These six slices seem to cover everything pretty well—all the features in the ball seem to fit nicely into one slice or another. But, we've seen everything from two slices (conventions and everything else) to nine slices (all the traits in the Six-Trait Model plus

> **BOX 2.1   Scavenger Hunt**
>
> Additional examples of holistic and analytical trait rubrics are presented in the Resource section. See if you can find examples of each.

dividing the trait of conventions into grammar, spelling, capitalization, and punctuation).

How many slices? Holistic = keep the ball whole. Analytical Trait = slice the ball up in ways that assist teachers and students to visualize and discuss the important components and how they fit together. There is no single number of traits that will do this; it depends on the complexity of the skill or product.

Which Type of Rubric Is Best?

Answer: It depends. Since these are scoring "tools," they should be selected and used based on the job at hand. Each type has strengths and limitations.

Holistic rubrics are well-suited for the following purposes:

- Judging simple products or performances—ones that really don't have more than one trait of importance, such as reading fluency or response to an essay question asking about knowledge of the potassium cycle in the cell

- Getting a quick snapshot of overall quality or achievement and thus are often used in large-scale assessments (national, state, or district levels) to quickly evaluate a large number of student responses

- Judging the "impact" of a product or performance (e.g., to what extent was the essay persuasive? did the play entertain?). Examples of this are the NAEP writing rubrics in the Resource section. The NAEP provides a separate, holistic rubric for three types of writing—narrative, persuasive, and expository (see definition in Box 2.2). Each rubric is intended to score the overall success of the piece of writing in accomplishing its primary purpose. How well is a story told (narrative)? How well does a piece persuade (persuasive)? Or how well does a piece explain (expository)?

But, despite these advantages, holistic rubrics have their downside:

- There is no detailed analysis of the strengths and weaknesses of a product or performance. So, they're not as useful diagnostically to help plan instruction. Nor do they provide students with detailed feedback to guide their improvement. Two students can receive the same score for vastly different reasons. Does an overall rating of "3" on a 4-point holistic writing rubric mean that a student

> **BOX 2.2 Definition: Primary Trait Rubrics**
>
> The "technical" term for this NAEP-type rubric is "primary trait." You score only the most telling, or primary, trait in the performance.

> **BOX 2.3**   Advantages of Breaking Down a Complex Performance Into
> Component Parts
>
>   **Playing the Violin**
>
> I (Judith Arter) play the violin. I had a teacher who wanted to make sure
> I got my money's worth during my lesson. So, she would point out
> everything that made a passage sound less than optimum—bowing a
> little too close to the bridge or not parallel to the bridge; playing the
> passage in second position rather than in first; leading with the thumb; paying at-
> tention to a couple of the notes that are fuzzy; pressing down more on the bow at a
> particular point in the passage, and so on. I would much rather have had her tell
> me the two things to work on first.
>
> Violin playing is a complex performance. It needs to be broken down into doable
> components that can be practiced separately before they can be combined into the
> final product. For example, it is extremely useful to practice in the following manner.
> First, just concentrate on keeping the bow straight—don't worry about your wrist or
> if the notes are in tune. Then just concentrate on keeping a straight wrist—don't
> worry about your bow or the notes being in tune. Next, just concentrate on the
> notes—don't worry about your wrist or bow. Finally, try all three things together.

has demonstrated strong idea development ("4") and weak use of conventions ("2"), or vice-versa? Without more specific feedback, it is difficult for the student to know exactly what to do to improve.

Analytical rubrics overcome some of the limitations of holistic rubrics.
They are better suited for the following purposes:

- Judging complex performances (e.g., research process) involving several significant dimensions (e.g., identifying a research question, using
  various research skills, synthesizing information from multiple
  sources, drawing conclusions). By breaking such performances down
  into traits, raters (including students and teachers) can more readily
  grasp the essential components of quality.

- Providing more specific information or feedback to students, parents,
  and teachers about the strengths and weaknesses of a performance.
  Teachers can use the information provided by analytic evaluation to
  target instruction to particular areas of need. From an instructional
  perspective, analytical trait rubrics help students come to better
  understand the nature of quality work since they identify the important dimensions of a product or performance. Examples of this are
  given in Box 2.3.

BOX 2.3   Continued

Golf

"One of the best examples of good teaching I have ever encountered was with a golf professional. On my first lesson, he said, 'Here is a bucket of balls . . . hit 'em.' A few minutes later he wandered back and quietly said, 'Keep hitting them, only this time keep your head down, eye on the ball.' By the next bucket of balls he had introduced one more skill for the day . . . no more. Before a few weeks were out, he had quietly attended to my feet, grip, shoulder level, and follow through. A few years later I realized with a start that every single one of my problems was visible on the first lesson. If I had attended to all of them that first day, I would probably have missed the ball entirely and resigned in disgust from ever playing golf again."

> —*Donald Graves. (1983). Writing: Teacher & Children at Work Portsmouth, NH: Heinemann.*

Writing

Good writing requires sound ideas, organized in an appropriate manner, with a voice appropriate for the audience and purpose, using words wisely and well, with appropriate sentences, and intentional conventions. That is a lot for students to attend to all at once, especially if they have no vocabulary for talking about these things. Analytical trait scoring guides provide the language and the focus for discussing complex skills, so the essential component parts can be practiced separately.

There is, of course, a trade-off. Analytical trait rubrics are typically more time-consuming to learn and apply—after all, you have more to discern— and more likely to yield lower agreement among different raters (at least at first) because there are several traits to be considered. Thus, analytic scoring may be less desirable for use in large-scale assessment contexts, where speed and reliability are essential.

Holistic and Analytical Trait—The Bottom Line

Although there are no hard-and-fast rules, we generally recommend the use of analytical trait rubrics for day-to-day classroom use, where ongoing assessment is integrated with instruction and where specific feedback is needed to guide improvement of teaching and learning (but see Box 2.4).

BOX 2.4   Misconception Alert!

Analytical trait systems are not worth the effort in the classroom if all they are to be used for is putting grades on student papers. If, however, they are used as an instructional methodology—to focus instruction, communicate with students, allow for student self-evaluation, and direct instruction on traits—they are very powerful.

You may be thinking, "I don't want to use an analytical trait rubric because I don't want to have to score all traits on every assignment." If you are thinking this, then we have good news. You don't have to! You can pick and choose the traits that make the most sense for individual assignments. For example, you might want to spend two weeks working just on the trait of "voice." Or, you might spend the first half of the semester teaching students the traits one by one. You would only begin scoring work on those traits after they've been taught. Or, you might find that "ideas" and "organization" are especially important for a particular assignment. Great! If so, you can weight them more heavily.

Rubrics are a tool. Use them in ways that make sense to accomplish the designated job.

Holistic scoring is most appropriate for summative and/or large-scale assessment, where an overall performance rating, rather than detailed feedback, is needed.

Holistic and analytical trait considerations are summarized in Figure 2.3.

Choice #2: Generic (General) or Task-Specific Rubrics?

A **generic (general) rubric** can be used across similar performances. You'd use the same rubric for judging *all* open-ended mathematics problems, *all* writing, *all* oral presentations, *all* critical thinking, or *all* group interaction. For example, the Six-Trait Writing rubric (Figure 2.2) may be used to judge many kinds of written products, irrespective of the writing task.

Task-specific rubrics are just that—each one can only be used for a single task (see the example in Figure 2.4).

Is it clear how the rubric is directly tied to the specific task in Figure 2.4? The rubric couldn't be used for any other task. In fact, the rubric would make no sense at all without the task.

Is it also clear that any of the generic mathematics rubrics (the mathematics rubric in Figure 2.1 or the Illinois or NWREL examples in the Resource section) could be used to score responses to the Olympics task, as well as a host of other problems in mathematics?

For this constructed-response assessment, choose a scoring method:

── Choose **Holistic** *OR* **Analytical Trait** ──

Holistic	
5	
4	✔
3	
2	
1	

Analytical Trait				
	Trait 1	Trait 2	Trait 3	Trait 4
5		✔		
4	✔			
3			✔	
2				✔
1				

Definition: One score or rating for the entire product or performance.

Examples: *California Mathematics* (see Figure 2.1 and the Resource section) and *Wauwatosa Developmental Continuum* (see Resource section)

When to Use

➡ Quick snapshot of overall status or achievement

➡ When speed of scoring is more important than knowing how to precisely describe quality

➡ Simple products or performance

Disadvantages

➡ Two students can get the same score for vastly different reasons

➡ Not as good for identifying strengths and weaknesses and planning instruction

➡ Not as useful for students to use

Definition: Several scores or ratings for a product or performance. Each score represents an important dimension or trait of the performance or product.

Examples: *Six-Trait Model in Writing* (see Figure 2.2 and Resource section) and *NWREL Mathematics* (see Resource section)

When to Use

➡ Planning instruction—shows relative strengths and weaknesses

➡ Teaching students the nature of a quality product or performance—they need the details

➡ Detailed feedback to students or parents

➡ When knowing how to precisely describe quality is more important than speed

➡ Complicated skills, products, or performances for which several dimensions are needed in order to be clear

Disadvantages

➡ Scoring is slower

➡ Takes longer to learn

Figure 2.3 Holistic or Analytical Trait?

Task: Joe, Sarah, Jose, Zabi, and Kim decided to hold their own Olympics after watching the Olympics on TV. . . . The children decided to have three events—frisbee toss, weight lift, and 50-yard dash. They also decided to make each event equally important. . . . The children's scores for each of the events are listed below:

Child	Frisbee Toss	Weight Lift	50-Yard Dash
Joe	40 yards	205 pounds	9.5 seconds
Jose	30 yards	170 pounds	8.0 seconds
Kim	45 yards	130 pounds	9.0 seconds
Sarah	28 yards	120 pounds	7.6 seconds
Zabi	48 yards	140 pounds	8.3 seconds

(a) Who would be the overall winner?

(b) Explain how you decided who would be the overall winner. Be sure to show all your work.

Rating Criteria

4 = accurate ranking of children on each event; citing Zabi as overall winner

3 = using a ranking approach but misinterpreting performance on the dash event and naming incorrect winner

2 = cites overall winner or a tie, with explanation that demonstrates recognition that a quantitative means of comparison is needed

1 = selection of overall winner with an irrelevant, nonquantitative, or no explanation

0 = no response

Figure 2.4. Task-Specific Rubric: Student Olympics
SOURCE: National Assessment of Educational Progress, 1992.

We can hear you thinking, "Why do I need to know this?" Actually, the distinction is essential, based, again, on intended use. If our main goal is scoring (generating a number), then task-specific rubrics might be easier to use. However, if our goal is to teach students about the nature of quality, then generic rubrics are more effective.

Here's why most teachers find generic rubrics useful:

- You don't need to develop (or learn) a new rubric for each task. Developing a quality rubric is difficult and time consuming. Given the frenzied life of most teachers, the thought of creating a rubric for each and every open-ended assignment or performance task is daunting, to say the least.

- Sometimes, you *can't* develop a new rubric for each task. When students are assembling portfolios, for example, they frequently select different pieces of work to demonstrate particular skills. Task-specific scoring would require a new rubric for every single piece of work. That would be inefficient and unnecessary.

    The National Assessment of Educational Progress ran into this problem in 1992. Before this time, they gave several specific writing prompts (topics) to students and scored them using task-specific rubrics. In 1992 they decided to ask students to self-select papers from their daily classroom work to supplement their standardized writing sample. Oops, can't do task-specific scoring—there are too many different topics. The result? The three generic rubrics in the Resource section.

- Generic rubrics are useful to help students understand the nature of quality—the "big picture" details that contribute to the quality of a type of performance or product. Task-specific rubrics only allow students to see what quality looks like in a single problem—the one at hand. The goal with generic rubrics is to help students see what quality looks like across similar tasks.

    General = generalize. We want students to apply what they learned about quality in one task to the next task—we want them to generalize. It is easier for students to learn a general rubric that can be applied to a number of similar tasks, such as an oral report or scientific investigation, than to try to figure out a new rubric for each task.

    In fact, we remember a high school social studies teacher who began with task-specific rubrics and then realized that she was putting the same general things in the rubric over and over again. Voilà! General traits emerged.

- Related to the point above, task-specific criteria *do not make the rater think*—the thinking has already been done for the rater. The developer of the rubric already thought through, for example, how good problem solving would look on *a particular* problem. Therefore, *the rater* doesn't have to think. Likewise, such criteria don't make students think. If a major reason for developing criteria is as a tool for learning in the classroom (e.g., students learn

> **BOX 2.5** Quote
>
> "The influencing of instructional practices to date has been served most powerfully by generic rubrics."
>
> —*Nidhi Khattri, Alison L. Reeve, and Rebecca J. Adamson, (1997), Studies of Educational Reform—Assessment of Student Performance (p. xx). Washington, DC: U.S. Office of Educational Research and Improvement (OERI).*

standards of quality for work), then generalized criteria do a better job because we want students to *think*—to be able to generalize what they learned on one task to make performance on the next task better.

- There can be more consistency between teachers. Rubrics help define the nature of quality in complex performances so that we're all looking at it in the same manner. This promotes "reliable" assessment across teachers, making subjective assessment more objective. In fact, rather than having teachers create their own rubrics independently, some schools or districts are supporting teachers to develop generic rubrics for collective use. Such a practice establishes a "standard" set of criteria and performance levels for classroom assessment, leading to greater consistency among teachers.

- It makes no sense to show task-specific criteria to students ahead of time because they "give away" the answer.

- What happens if a student comes up with a perfectly reasonable strategy or solution, but it isn't one included in the task-specific criteria? Have you ever been going fast through papers, using the scoring guide in the textbook and not really thinking about what you are doing? Sometimes, students can come up with perfectly reasonable answers, but you don't notice it. In fact, a personal communication from a major test publisher indicated that this is the reason why they are moving away from task-specific scoring—sometimes, students come up with reasonable responses, but they are marked incorrect because they are not in the task-specific rubric.

So, *why would anyone want to use a task-specific rubric?* There are some circumstances where you'll want to use them.

- It's easier and faster to get consistent scoring. It's easier to train a group of people to base scores on the presence or absence of, say, three specific facts than to train them to judge the extent to which students "understood the problem." Therefore, task-specific rubrics tend to be used in large-scale and "high stakes" contexts, such as state-level accountability assessments. So, if your main goal is to generate numbers, do task-specific scoring. It keeps costs down.

- Sometimes, you want to know whether students know particular facts, equations, methods, or procedures. Do students notice the three important sources of experimental error in a particular science experiment? Can students apply a specific algorithm in mathematics? Are students effectively using a particular painting technique in art? These specific features could be listed in the rubric descriptors for a particular task. So, task-specific scoring could happen in mathematics, social studies, science, and any class that has a particular content to be learned.

- In fact, in some circumstances you might want to have a combination of task-specific features and a generic trait or two. For example, consider a fitness plan in a high school health class. The teachers decided to look for the presence or absence of specific knowledge and relationships between ideas—task-specific components in a rubric. They also wanted to judge the quality of the writing using a generic rubric.

Task-Specific and Generic Rubrics—The Bottom Line

Generic rubrics are better for complex skills that generalize across tasks. Task-specific rubrics are better when you're looking for specific bits of information or use of a particular method. Task-specific and generic rubric considerations are summarized in Figure 2.5.

Choice #3: Number of Score Points

We've seen rubrics ranging from 3 to 7 points, although some developmental rubrics may extend over a larger range. Here are some examples:

- The Maryland Language Usage rubric (see Resource section) has a 3-point scale.
- The Massachusetts Oral Presentation rubric (see Resource section) has a 4-point scale.
- The Six-Trait Model in Writing (see Figure 2.2 and Resource section) has a 5-point scale.
- The California Mathematics rubric (see Figure 2.1 and Resource section) has a 6-point scale.
- The Wauwatosa Developmental Continuum (see Resource section) has 11 developmental levels.

How does one decide on a rubric scale? While there are no hard-and-fast rules, one needs to consider both the nature of the performance and the purpose for scoring. For example,

- What is a likely range of qualitatively different degrees of understanding, proficiency, or quality in the product or performance? Generally,

For these tasks (products or performances), choose a scoring method:

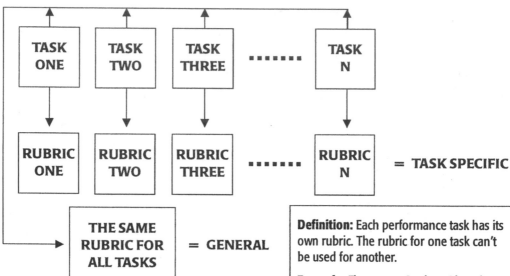

Definition: Similar performance tasks use the same rubric.

Examples: All the rubrics in the Resource section.

When to Use

→ When the rubric is being used instructionally to help students understand the nature of quality and generalize from one task to the next

→ When students will not all be doing exactly the same task; when students have a choice as to what evidence will be chosen to show competence on a particular skill or product

→ When teachers are trying to judge consistently in different classes or grades

Disadvantages

→ Takes longer to learn, but therein is also the strength—learning the rubrics is also learning the skill

→ Takes longer to score, when the only goal is to assess quickly

→ Sometimes, task-specific features have to be added if particular knowledge is desired

Definition: Each performance task has its own rubric. The rubric for one task can't be used for another.

Example: Figure 2.4–Student Olympics

When to Use

→ When speed of getting a score is more important than thinking through what is being scored

→ When you want to know if students know particular facts, equations, methods, or procedures

→ When consistency of scoring is of utmost importance

Disadvantages

→ Can't show to students ahead of time because it "gives away" the answer

→ Have to develop a new rubric for each task; this takes time and sometimes this isn't even possible (e.g., portfolios)

→ Does not make the rater think— scoring is on automatic pilot

→ "Right" answers not in the scoring guide are sometimes missed

→ Does not help define the nature of quality in general; only states what quality looks like for a particular task

Figure 2.5. Task-Specific or General?

the more open-ended and complex the performance, the broader the scale range.

- You need enough score points to distinguish quality (fewer than 4 is usually not enough), but not so many that teachers and students can't distinguish between the levels (more than 8 is usually too many except in developmental continuums where it is easy to see the progression over many levels).

- If the primary purpose of the rubric is to certify competence according to a standard, then many places use a 4-point scale, in which "3" is typically defined as the "standard," with "4" exceeding the standard. A "2" means just below the standard and a "1" means way below the standard.

- If a developmental rubric is employed to track student progress continuously across grade levels, a larger scale would be needed. To detect differences in quality in a single grade level, fewer points are needed.

- Some folks avoid an odd number of score points because of the tendency to "gravitate to the mean" (i.e., the middle score tends to become a "dumping ground"). However, other rubrics, like the Six-Trait Model, use a 5-point scale because the middle represents a "balance of strengths and weaknesses." The point here is that you must have a good reason for the scale you choose.

- Some teachers like to stay away from a 5-point scale because it looks too much like the typical A-F grading scale.

> **BOX 2.6** Scavenger Hunt
>
> Look in the Resource section for rubrics with different numbers of score points.

Number of Score Points—The Bottom Line

As with other design decisions, the number of score points depends on the purpose of the rubric and the nature of what is to be assessed. We recommend from 3 to 6 points for rubrics used to describe student achievement within a single grade level. If you have a developmental continuum—a rubric that stretches across grade levels and is designed to track student development on a skill—more points are used. We've seen 6 to 11 score points (levels) for rubrics that focus on a developmental continuum. To decide, ask yourself, "How many points are needed to adequately describe the range of performance I am seeing in student work?"

Chapter Summary

This chapter examined three ways that rubrics differ—holistic versus analytical trait; task-specific versus generic; and number of score points—and when to use each option. It is important to recognize that the categories aren't mutually exclusive—they're mix and match. You can have a holistic, generic 4-point rubric. Or you can have a task-specific, analytic rubric containing three traits and using a 5-point scale. Our goal is to enable the reader to identify the most appropriate scoring tool given the nature of the performance and the overall purpose of the assessment.

CHAPTER 3

Developing Rubrics

Guiding Question: *How do we design effective scoring rubrics?*

Where do these wonderful rubrics come from? How do we know that we have chosen the "right" performance criteria? How does one go about developing an effective rubric? In this chapter, we examine these questions and offer a tried-and-true process for identifying criteria and developing rubrics.

Getting Started

Developing a scoring rubric is challenging work, but it doesn't have to be onerous. Consider the following tips when getting started in developing or refining a rubric. These tips are also outlined visually in Figure 3.1. The visual icons from Figure 3.1 are repeated in the tips below to make it easy to relate the picture to the words.

- If you're an expert on the features of a high-quality product or performance, just list the criteria based on your experience— . Then fine-tune your list by using the criteria to actually

  score student work— . This never fails to remind one of subtle features that were initially overlooked.

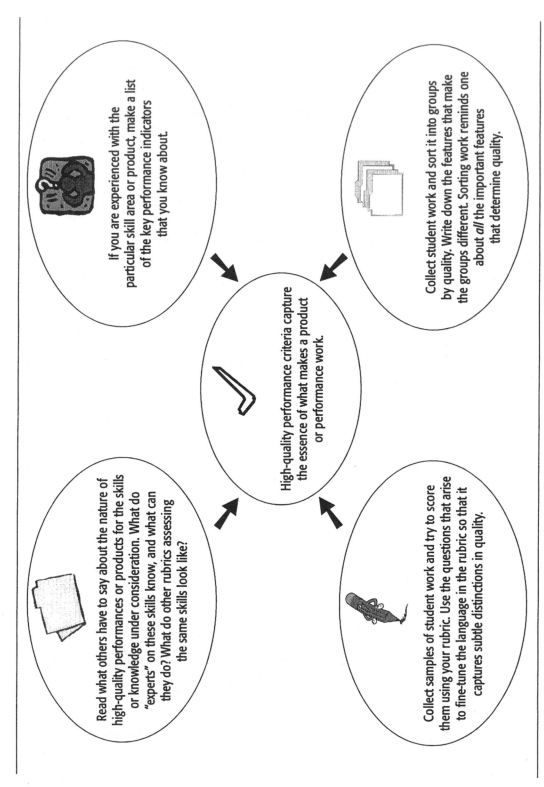

If you are experienced with the particular skill area or product, make a list of the key performance indicators that you know about.

Collect student work and sort it into groups by quality. Write down the features that make the groups different. Sorting work reminds one about *all* the important features that determine quality.

High-quality performance criteria capture the essence of what makes a product or performance work.

Read what others have to say about the nature of high-quality performances or products for the skills or knowledge under consideration. What do "experts" on these skills know, and what can they do? What do other rubrics assessing the same skills look like?

Collect samples of student work and try to score them using your rubric. Use the questions that arise to fine-tune the language in the rubric so that it captures subtle distinctions in quality.

Figure 3.1 How to Identify Performance Criteria

34

- If you have an intuitive sense of the features of a quality performance or product, sort student work into three or four groups based on level of quality— . Check your intuitive notion by reading the professional literature— , and fine-tune your criteria by scoring additional samples of student work— .

- Let's say you have no idea where to begin—you're not sure you could even sort student work into groups by level of quality. In this case, you need to start by reviewing the professional literature on the skills you are trying to assess to see what others have to say about expert performance— . For example, what does the professional literature say expert critical thinking looks like? Use these sources to develop or adapt draft criteria and then fine-tune them by sorting— and scoring additional samples— .

- You usually don't have to start from scratch. Always beg, borrow, steal, and adapt using existing rubrics as models— . But, even when using someone else's rubric, *always* engage in sorting and scoring— and— for three main reasons.

  First, it's just human nature that when we use criteria to sort and score student work, we come to better understand and "own" the criteria rather than seeing them as arbitrary guidelines imposed from an outside source. It becomes clear that the criteria we're generating or modifying are what we, ourselves, actually do value when we look at student work.

BOX 3.1   Sources for Rubrics

Appendix A in this book

Chicago Public Schools. (1994). *The CPS Performance Assessment Idea Book.* (Available from Chicago Public Schools, 1819 Pershing Road, Chicago, IL 60609)

Robert Marzano, Debra Pickering, and Jay McTighe. (1993). *Assessing Outcomes: Performance Assessment Using the Dimensions of Learning Model.* (Available from Association of Supervision and Curriculum Development, 1703 N. Beauregard Street, Alexandria, VA 22311; telephone 1-800-933-2723)

National Council of Supervisors of Mathematics. (1996). *Great Tasks and More!* (Available from the author at P.O. Box 10667, Golden, CO 80401; telephone 303-274-5932)

Regional Educational Laboratories. (1998). *Improving Classroom Assessment: A Toolkit for Professional Developers* (Appendix A). (Available from Northwest Regional Educational Laboratory, 101 SW Main, Suite 500, Portland, OR 97204; telephone 503-275-9500)

Second, it's a big time saver that someone else has already tried to describe performance levels in writing.

Third, rubrics obtained from others are most often also "works in progress" and will benefit from additional refinement.

- **Always** have samples of student work to look at. Armchair criteria, without the additional test of using them on actual student work, are usually weak criteria. Teachers ground their opinions or questions about indicators of quality by holding up a student work sample and saying "But, look at this one."

With these overall suggestions in mind, we're going to examine, with three specific examples, a typical process for identifying performance criteria and using them in the design of a scoring rubric.

Examples of Rubric Development

In the running examples below, we'll use the rubric-development procedure that begins with sorting student work——proceeds by looking at sample performance criteria from other places——and finishes with refinement of the rubric based on scoring——. (Remember, this was one of the options presented in the "tips" list above. It's actually the most frequently used option, that's why we're expanding on it here.)

Table 3.1 Samples of Student Performance to Collect

Self-Reflection	*Math Problem Solving*	*Writing*
Collect things that students have written in answer to questions like "Select a piece of work that you feel illustrates your best effort. Why did you select this piece?" "What does the piece you selected show about you as a _____?" (The blank would be filled by: writer, math problem solver, lifelong learner, or whatever skill students are self-reflecting about.) Other questions that might elicit student self-reflection might be "How have you changed this year in your ability to _____?" or "What do you currently understand about _____? What do you still need to understand?"	Collect samples of student open-ended problem solving. Remember that the task must really require students to problem solve and not just repeat memorized solutions to previously encountered problems.	Collect a variety of writing samples across grade levels for the desired type(s) of writing you want to examine (narrative, expository, and/or persuasive).

To illustrate the process in action, we'll present three running examples—mathematical problem solving, writing, and self-reflection letters. (Remember, we're developing performance criteria in order that we, and our students, have a clearer vision of the nature of quality. We're not necessarily doing it so we can "grade." This is especially a concern by teachers when developing criteria for self-reflection letters.)

> **BOX 3.2**   Reference
>
> This discussion was adapted from **Activity, 2.1,** Regional Educational Laboratories, *Improving Classroom Assessment: A Toolkit for Professional Developers,* February 1998, Northwest Regional Educational Laboratory, 101 SW Main, Suite 500, Portland, OR 97204; phone 503-275-9500.

Step 1: Gather Samples of Student Performance

Gather samples of student performance that illustrate the skill or behavior in question (see Table 3.1).

Step 2: Sort Student Work Into Groups and Write Down Reasons

Place the samples of student work into three piles: strong, middle, and weak. For the self-reflection example there might be three piles that illustrate levels of sophistication with respect to self-reflection. As the student work is sorted, write down reasons for placing pieces in the various stacks. In other words, if a piece is placed in the "sophisticated" pile, why? What cues you that the work is sophisticated? What are you saying to yourself as you place a piece of work into a pile? What might you say to a student as you return this work? Answers to these questions reveal criteria (see Figure 3.1).

Keep sorting work until you are not adding anything new to your list of attributes. Try to create as large and diverse a list as possible. Recent lists have included such things as those shown in Table 3.2.

Put in specific details—they're very helpful both to remind yourself and your colleagues what you meant and to develop student-friendly versions of the criteria. It's the specific comments such as "the student started out well but seemed to get lost in the middle" rather than the general comments such as "logical" that will be most helpful. Continually challenge yourself to "say more about that" or "what specific things done by the student were cues that the student used a logical process?" Continually challenge yourself to think beyond general words such as "voice," "perceptive," and "good communication." Students don't understand what is meant by those words. Since the criteria are supposed to increase student understanding of the features of quality, we need to be clear on the indicators in the work that cue our judgments of quality. Also, challenging yourself to "identify the specific indicators in the student work that made me judge it logical" causes you to refine your own understanding of what you mean by these terms (but see Boxes 3.3 and 3.4).

> **BOX 3.3   CAUTION! Negative Wording**
>
> Sometimes this procedure leads to very negative phrases at the low end of the scale, such as "clueless" and "totally wrong." One way to avoid this is to think about the comments you would actually make to students when you hand back work—make "I" statements, such as "I was confused as to what you did" and "I would like to know more about why you used the numbers you did."

Thinking about grading while placing work in stacks has an added benefit—it clarifies the connection between grades and the features of student work that earn the grade, thereby removing some of the subjectivity from grading.

Table 3.2 Examples of Attributes

	Self-Reflection	Mathematics	Writing
High	Detailed; many things covered; insightful; self-revelation; examples provided; the student seemed motivated; sets goals for the future; looks at more than one thing; considers content as well as process; takes risks; accurate; discussion is related to criteria; growth supported with examples; organized well; sincere; honest; there are comparisons over time; shares feelings; looks at both strengths and weaknesses; there is depth to the analysis; there are good reasons and explanations; revealing; voice; easy to read; looks at skill improvement; there is ownership; there is a personal reaction; it is specific; it looks ahead; it is thorough; ideas are synthesized; it is readable; it is neat	I can tell exactly what the student did at every step; concise and to the point; correct answer, logical and sequential; good explanation; precise; correct labels; explains thought process; supports reasoning; correct answer Appropriate use of pictures, diagrams, and symbols; used the right numbers in the right order; sequencing was purposeful; evidence that the answer was checked for reasonableness; I could tell exactly what the student did and why he or she did it	I want to keep reading; insightful; I can easily follow the train of thought; funny; interesting; good opening; good pacing; good closing; nice use of words; flows; has a point to make; is individual; varied sentence lengths; varied sentence beginnings; conventions done correctly

(continued)

Table 3.2 Continued

	Self-Reflection	Mathematics	Writing
Middle	Shows then hides; beginning of ownership; two-dimensional; some specifics; describes performance but leaves a lot out; few insights; focuses on only a few things; considers content or process but not both; is somewhat accurate; doesn't seem completely honest; there are descriptions of individual pieces of work but no comparisons over time; I have to make some inferences as to what the student meant	Right idea, but computational errors; forgot a step, but the rest is OK; didn't go far enough; didn't clarify; one has to make some inferences as to what the student did; doesn't show all the steps; used correct data but incorrect process; used correct process but incorrect data	The topic is broad, but I can see where the writer is going; support is attempted; I have some questions; the theme is not entirely clear; I can follow it, but the pacing seems off; the beginning or ending could be better; words are correct but don't have flair; words are sometimes used incorrectly; sentences are correct but not lively; conventions are mostly correct
Low	Vague; simple restatements; mechanical; focuses mainly on surface features; obvious; same old same old; no examples; purposeless; I like it/I don't like it; one-dimensional; superficial; does not seem to be aware of the need to set goals; takes no risks; doesn't seem honest; is not accurate; there seems to be no ownership; I can't follow what the student is trying to say; hard to read; not organized well	I couldn't follow the sequence; the answer doesn't look reasonable; used wrong numbers; used the wrong process; mixed processes; shooting in the dark; illogical; unclear; no explanation of answer; I had to make a lot of inferences as to what the student did; I was confused by the explanation	This is just a list; there is no theme; I can't follow this; everything seems as important as everything else; this is repetitious; it's boring; the writer seems indifferent; the writing is lifeless; there is no point of view; the words are very general; words are used incorrectly; word choice detracts from the message; phrasing seems awkward; all the sentences are the same length; it's choppy; there are lots of errors in spelling, capitalization, etc.

> **Box 3.4   Sorting: Task Specific or Generic Criteria**
>
> When sorting certain kinds of student work, like mathematics, you might find your-self listing "task specific" criteria as well as the general comments emphasized so far in this chapter. For example, you might note that in a strong response the student "adds up the numbers for the two kinds of fruit and then subtracts the number of students."
>
> This is good! Sometimes we want task-specific criteria, and sometimes we want general criteria. Generating both when sorting work really helps one to see and understand the difference.

Step 3: Cluster the Reasons Into "Traits" or Important Dimensions of Performance

The sorting process used thus far in this exercise is "holistic." Participants end up with a list of comments for high, medium, and low performance; any single paper gets only one overall score.

Usually during the listing of comments someone will say something to the effect that "I had trouble placing this paper into one stack or another because it was strong on reasoning but weak on communication." This provides an excellent teachable moment to bring up the *reasons for analytical trait scoring systems*—scoring each student work sample along more than one dimension. The reasons are that (a) it better shows a profile of student strengths and weaknesses, (b) it assists students to be better able to discuss their own work, and (c) novices often can't improve all parts of the performance at one time—this helps break the performance down into teachable segments. Besides, we, as teachers, feel more comfortable being able to commend students for the strengths in their work, even if there are also some weaknesses.

To develop "traits" (important dimensions of performance), you can identify comments on the brainstormed list that seem to go together and indicate which comments relate to each trait at the high, middle, and low levels. For example, people frequently see the traits of communication, problem solving/reasoning, mathematical understanding, and correct computation when sorting math work (see Figure 3.2). Number these traits 1, 2, 3, and 4. Then go through your comments and place them into the categories. Put the trait number next to each comment on the brainstormed list.

For example, in math the trait of **Communication** might include at the HIGH level "I can tell exactly what the student did at every step," "good explanation," "clearly explains thought process," and "I had to make very few inferences about what the student did and why he or she did it."

Self-Reflection	*Mathematics*	*Writing*
1. Skill Analysis	1. Conceptual Understanding	1. Ideas/Content
2. Sincerity	2. Strategies/Reasoning	2. Organization
3. Goal Setting	3. Computation/Execution	3. Voice
4. Presentation	4. Insights	4. Word Choice
	5. Communication	5. Sentence Fluency
		6. Conventions
		7. Presentation

Figure 3.2. Common Traits

As another example, **Skill Analysis** for self-reflection at the HIGH level might include "detailed," "many things covered," "insightful," "examples provided," "looks at more than one thing," "considers content as well as process," "accurate," "discussion related to criteria," "growth supported with examples," "looks at both strengths and weaknesses," "depth of analysis," "revealing," "specific," "thorough," and "synthesized ideas."

Common traits for our three running examples are shown in Figure 3.2.

Make sure that your "traits" cover everything of importance. Be prepared for frequent changes, at least at the initial stages of building the rubric. Ideas need time to gel. We get new perspectives and insights as we attempt to "make sense" of our criteria.

Don't go to extremes with this. Just keep going until you are comfortable that you have an agreed-on list of key traits and attributes.

Then compare your list of valued features to local or state content standards that correspond to the type of work sorted. What similarities do you find? There are always lots of overlaps—after all, the content standards were developed to represent the outcomes we all value for students. Matching your traits to content standards helps clarify how standards are represented in the daily work of students. It's also a relief to see that content standards represent what we already value as outcomes for students; it's not new.

Look at similarities between your list of valued qualities and the statements in rubrics developed by others (see the Resource section). There are always many similarities because, after all, how different can lists of quality criteria be? This demonstrates that, if done well, scoring criteria are not pulled out of a hat; they represent what we all already value in student work—someone has just taken the time to write it down. If everything is done well, there will be alignment between (a) what we value in student work, (b) content standards, and (c) the way the content standards are assessed.

Step 4: Write a Value-Neutral Definition of Each Trait

Write a definition of each trait. For example:

Sincerity reflects how serious the student is about the self-reflection process. It is the degree of ownership, effort, and honesty in the self-reflection. It is the degree to which the student makes a real effort to self-analyze.

These definitions should be "value neutral"—that is, they describe what the trait is about, not what good performance looks like. (Descriptions of *good* performance on the trait are left to the descriptors under the "high" rating.) Here is an example of the definition above converted to a statement that is *not* value neutral:

Sincerity is taking ownership for work, really trying hard, and being very honest; the student has made a sincere effort to self-reflect.

Step 5: Find Samples of Student Performance
That Illustrate Each Score Point on Each Trait

Find samples of student work that are good examples of strong, weak, and mid-range performance on each trait. Be sure to have several samples representing typical ranges of performance at each level of schooling: early elementary, late elementary, middle school, and high school. These samples are variously called "anchors," "models," "range finders," and "exemplars."

These samples help scorers practice consistent scoring. They also equip students to engage in more accurate and productive self-assessment. By providing tangible illustrations of the rubric descriptors, the potentially ambiguous language of a rubric is exemplified, aiding everyone to see what "good" looks like.

Important hint: Have more than a single example. If you show students only one example of what a good performance looks like, all your students will copy it, as Box 3.5 illustrates.

BOX 3.5 Vignette: You Need More Than One Sample to Illustrate Each Level on the Rubric

During a recent writing assessment, every paper from a classroom began with "I see you there . . . ." It was obvious that the teacher had only shown the students one sample of a high-quality paper—the one that begins "I see you there Evan Blake."

Since we frequently use this paper in writing workshops to illustrate the sound use of sentence fragments, we knew exactly which paper had been used.

Step 6: Continuously Refine

Criteria and rubrics evolve with use. Try them out. You'll probably find some parts of the rubric that work fine and some that don't. Add and modify descriptions so that they communicate better. Choose better sample papers that illustrate what you mean. Revise traits if you need to. Let students help—this is, after all, a tool for learning.

Chapter Summary

This chapter illustrated how to develop rubrics. Boxes 3.6 and 3.7 summarize the major points.

BOX 3.6   Summary Thoughts

■ The procedures in this chapter are targeted at developing rubrics for use in the classroom as instructional tools, although many of the same principles hold for any rubric used in any setting.

■ The same procedure can be used to develop holistic or analytical trait scoring guides; task-specific or general scoring guides.

■ Detail is the key—go beyond general terminology like "logical" and "understands the problem." What are the indicators of "logical"?

■ Always have more than a single sample of student work to illustrate each level on your rubric.

■ Let students help!

BOX 3.7   Steps in Developing Scoring Guides, Rubrics, and Performance Criteria

■ *Read the literature* on what people skilled in doing "X" look like (where "X" is the skill or knowledge that is to assessed—for example, writing, critical thinking, group skills, science process skills, math problem solving). This will give you ideas on how experts differ from novices on the skill in question, which in turn helps focus you on the attributes that most distinguish quality performance.

■ *Beg, borrow and steal rubrics* developed by others. This will give you good ideas on what others have seen as indicators of quality performance.

■ *Gather samples of student work and sort it into groups* by quality. Describe what makes the group different. This will help conceptualize the features of work that contribute to its quality. Always do this—it contributes to local ownership.

■ *Score samples of student work.* Work on attaining consistency between raters through dialogue. Always do this—it will add detail and fine distinctions to the rubric.

CHAPTER 4

A Rubric for Rubrics—or— It's Metarubric Time

Guiding Question: *How will we know when we have an effective rubric?*

There is no single correct way to develop and use rubrics; however, there *are* some wrong ways. This chapter explores what we, and others, have discovered should always be true of rubrics and things that developers should avoid. We'll include common mistakes made by beginners.

A Rubric for Rubrics

Since rubrics are complex products, and rubric writing is a complex skill, it's useful to have a means to discuss features of quality. To this end, we will "walk the talk" and offer a rubric for evaluating the quality of rubrics—a metarubric, if you will (see Figure 4.1). Please notice that the definitions of the metarubric traits used in the text below are also reproduced in Figure 4.1. We did this in case you want to copy the metarubric (Figure 4.1) for use when you are evaluating the quality of the rubrics you are using.

The rubric for rubrics is analytical, consisting of four traits—Content, Clarity, Practicality, and Technical Soundness. It uses a 3-point scale, where 3 = "ready to roll," 2 = "on its way but needs revision," and 1 = "not ready for prime time."

Please note that **this metarubric was developed for classroom assessments,** not for large-scale assessments. Although many of the features for large-scale assessment rubrics would be the same, some traits might need to be modified, added, or deleted for this use.

(text continues on p. 52)

Metarubric Trait 1: Content/Coverage

The content of a rubric defines what to look for in a student's product or performance to determine its quality. Rubric content truly is the final definition of content standards because the rubric describes what will "count." Regardless of what is stated in content standards, curriculum frameworks, or instructional materials, the content of the rubric is what teachers and students will use to determine what they need to do in order to succeed—what they see is what you'll get. Therefore, it is essential that the rubric cover all essential aspects that define quality in a product or performance and leaves out all things trivial.

If a rubric contains things other than those that really distinguish quality, teachers won't buy into them, students will not learn what really contributes to quality, and you might find yourself having to score down work that you feel in your heart is strong or give good ratings to work you feel in your heart is weak.

When evaluating a rubric for content, ask yourself these questions: Can I explain why each thing I have included in my rubric is essential to a quality performance? Can I cite references that describe the best thinking in the field on the nature of quality performance? Can I describe what I left out, and why I left it out? Do I ever find performances or products that are scored low (or high) that I really think are good (or bad)? Is this worth the time devoted to it?

Ready to Roll

- There is justification for the dimensions of student performance or work that are cited as being indicators of quality. Content is based on the best thinking in the field.
- The content has the "ring of truth"—your experience as a teacher confirms that the content is truly what you *do* look for when you evaluate the quality of student work or performance.
- If counting the number of something (such as the number of references at the end of a research report) is included as an indicator, such counts really *are* indicators of quality. (Sometimes, for example, 2 really good references are better than 10 bad ones. Or, in writing, 10 errors in spelling all on different words is more of a problem than a single spelling error on the same word used 10 times.)
- The relevant emphasis on various features of performance is right—things that are more important are stressed more; things that are less important are stressed less.
- Definitions of terms are correct—they reflect current thinking in the field.
- The number of points used in the rating scale make sense. In other words, if a 5-point scale is used, is it clear why? Why not a 4- or 6-point scale? The level of precision is appropriate for the use.
- The developer has been selective yet complete. There is a sense that the features of importance have been covered well; yet there is no overload.
- You are left with few questions about what was included or why it was included.
- The rubric is insightful. It helps you organize your thinking about what it means to perform with quality. The content helps you assist students understand the nature of quality.

Figure 4.1. Metarubric

SOURCE: © 2000, Assessment Training Institute. Used with permission.

On Its Way but Needs Revision

■ The rubric is about halfway there on content. Much of the content is relevant, but you can easily think of some important things that have been left out or that have been given short shrift.

■ The developer is beginning to identify the relevant aspects of performance. You can see where the rubric is headed, even though some features might not ring true or are out of balance.

■ Although much of the rubric seems reasonable, some of it doesn't seem to represent current best thinking about what it means to perform well on the product or skill under consideration.

■ Although the content seems fairly complete, the rubric sprawls—it's not organized very well.

■ Although much of the rubric covers that which is important, it also contains several irrelevant features that might lead to an incorrect conclusion about the quality of the students' performance.

Not Ready for Prime Time

■ You can think of many important dimensions of a quality performance or product that are not included in the rubric.

■ There are several irrelevant features. You find yourself asking, "Why assess this?" or "Why should this count?" or "Why is it important that students do it *this* way?"

■ Content is based on counting the number of something when quality is more important than quantity.

■ The rubric seems "mixed up"—things that go together don't seem to be placed together. Things that are different are put together.

■ The rubric is very much out of balance—features of importance are weighted incorrectly. (For example, a business letter might have several categories that relate to format but only one that relates to content and organization.)

■ Definitions of terms are incorrect—they don't reflect current best thinking in the field.

■ The rubric is an endless list of seemingly everything the developer can think of that might be even marginally important. There is no organization to it. The developer seems unable to pick out that which is most significant or telling. The rubric looks like a brainstormed list.

■ You are left with many questions about what was included and why it was included.

■ There are many features of the rubric that might lead a rater to an incorrect conclusion about the quality of a student's performance.

■ The rubric doesn't seem to align with the content standard it's supposed to assess.

(continued)

Figure 4.1. Continued
SOURCE: © 2000, Assessment Training Institute. Used with permission.

Metarubric Trait 2: Clarity

A rubric is clear to the extent that teachers, students, and others are likely to interpret the statements and terms in the rubric the same way. Please notice that a rubric can be strong on the trait of content/coverage, but weak on the trait of clarity—the rubric seems to cover the important dimensions of performance, but they aren't described very well. Likewise, a rubric can be strong on the trait of clarity, but weak on the trait of content/coverage—it's very clear what the rubric means, it's just not very important stuff.

Questions to ask yourself when evaluating a rubric for clarity are these: Would two teachers be likely to give the same rating on a product or performance? Could I find examples of student work or performances that illustrate each level of quality? Could I show someone else sample student work or performances that specifically illustrate each score point on each dimension?

Ready to Roll

- The rubric is so clear that different teachers would give the same rating to the same product or performance.
- A single teacher could use the rubric to provide consistent ratings across assignments, time, and students.
- Words are specific and accurate. It is easy to understand just what is meant.
- There are several samples of student products or performance that illustrate each score point. It is clear why each sample was scored the way it was.
- Terms are defined.
- There is just enough descriptive detail in the form of concrete indicators, adjectives, and descriptive phrases that allow you to match a student performance to the "right" score.
- There is not an overabundance of descriptive detail—the developer seems to have a sense of that which is most telling.
- The basis for assigning ratings or checkmarks is clear. Each score point is defined with indicators and descriptions.

On Its Way but Needs Revision

- Major headings are defined, but there is little detail to assist the rater to choose the proper score points.
- There is some attempt to define terms and include descriptors, but it doesn't go far enough.
- Teachers would agree on how to rate some things in the rubric while others are not well-defined and would probably result in disagreements.
- A single teacher would probably have trouble being consistent in scoring across students or assignments.

Figure 4.1. Continued

Not Ready for Prime Time

- Language is so vague that almost anything could be meant. You find yourself saying things like "I'm confused" or "I don't have any idea what they mean by this."
- There are no definitions for terms used in the rubric or the definitions don't help or are incorrect.
- The rubric is little more that a list of categories to rate followed by a rating scale. Nothing is defined. Few descriptors are given to define levels of performance.
- No sample student work is provided that illustrates what is meant.
- Teachers are unlikely to agree on ratings because there are so many different ways a descriptor can be interpreted.
- The only way to distinguish levels is words like "extremely," "very," "some," "little," and "none" or "completely," "substantially," "fairly well," "little," and "not at all."

Metarubric Trait 3: Practicality

Having clear criteria that cover the right "stuff" means nothing if the system is too cumbersome to use. The trait of practicality refers to ease of use—can teachers and students understand and use it easily? Does it give them the information they need for instructional decision making and tracking student progress toward important learning outcomes? Can the rubric be used for more than just a way to assess students? Can it also be used to improve the very achievement also being assessed?

Ready to Roll

- The rubric is manageable—there are not too many things to remember; teachers and students can easily internalize them.
- It is clear how to translate results into instruction. For example, if students appear to be weak in writing, is it clear what should be taught to improve performance?
- The rubric is usually analytical trait rather than holistic when the product or skill is complex.
- The rubric is usually general rather than task specific. In other words, the rubric is broadly applicable to the content of interest; it is not tied to any specific exercise or assignment.
- If task-specific and/or holistic rubrics are used, their justification is clear and appropriate. Justifications could include (a) the complexity of the skill being assessed—a "big" skill would require an analytical trait rubric while a "small skill" might only need a single "holistic" rubric; or (b) the nature of the skill being assessed—understanding a concept might require a task-specific rubric while demonstrating a skill (such as an oral presentation) might imply a general rubric.
- The rubric can be used by students themselves to revise their own work, plan their own learning, and track their own progress. There is assistance on how to use the rubric in this fashion.

(continued)

Figure 4.1. Continued

- There are "student friendly" versions.
- The rubric is so clear that a student doing poorly would know exactly what to do in order to improve.
- The rubric is visually appealing to students; it draws them into its use.
- The rubric is divided into easily understandable chunks (traits) that help students grasp the essential aspects of a complex performance.
- The language used in the rubric is developmental—low scores do not imply "bad" or "failure."

On Its Way but Needs Revision

- The rubric might provide useful information but might not be easy to use.
- The rubric might be holistic when to be of maximal use, an analytical trait rubric would be better.
- The rubric has potential for teacher use but would need some "tweaking"—combining long lists of attributes into traits or adjusting the language so it is clear what is intended.
- The rubric has potential for student self-use but would need some "tweaking"—including wording changes, streamlining, or making the format more appealing.
- Students could accurately rate their own work or performances, but it might not be clear to them what to do to improve.
- Although there are some problems, it would be easier to try and fix the rubric than look elsewhere.

Not Ready for Prime Time

- There is no justification given for the type of rubric used—holistic or analytical trait, task-specific or generic. You get the feeling that the developer didn't know what options were available and just did what seemed like a good idea at the time.
- There seems to be no consideration of how the rubric might be useful to teachers. The intent seems to be only large-scale assessment efficiency.
- The rubric is not manageable—there is an overabundance of things to rate—it would take forever; or everything is presented all at once and might overwhelm the user.
- It is not clear how to translate results into instruction.
- The rubric is worded in ways that students would not understand.
- Fixing the rubric for student use would be harder than looking elsewhere.

Metarubric Trait 4: Technical Quality

It is important to have "hard" evidence that the performance criteria adequately measure the goal being assessed, that it can be applied consistently, and that there is reason to believe that the ratings actually do represent what students can do.

Figure 4.1. Continued

SOURCE: © 2000, Assessment Training Institute. Used with permission.

Although this might be beyond the scope of what individual classroom teachers can do, we all still have the responsibility to ask hard questions when we adopt or develop a rubric. The following are the kinds of things all educators should think about.

Ready to Roll

- There is technical information associated with the rubric that describes rater agreement rates and the conditions under which such agreement rates can be obtained. These rater agreement rates are at least 65% exact agreement and 98% within one point.
- The language used in the rubric is appropriate for the diversity of students found in typical classrooms. The language avoids stereotypic thinking, appeals to various learning styles, and uses language that ELL students would understand.
- There have been formal bias reviews of rubric content, studies of ratings under the various conditions in which ratings will occur, and studies, that, for example, handwriting and gender or race of the student doesn't affect judgment, etc.
- Wording is supportive of students—it describes status of a performance rather than judgments of student worth.

On Its Way but Needs Revision

- There is technical information associated with the rubric that describes rater agreement rates and the conditions under which such agreement rates can be obtained. These rater agreement rates aren't, however, at the levels described under "ready to roll." But, this might be due to less than adequate training of raters rather than to the scale itself.
- The language used in the rubric is inconsistent in its appropriateness for the diversity of students found in typical classrooms, but these problems can be easily corrected.
- The authors present some hard data on the technical soundness of the rubric, but this has holes.
- Wording is inconsistently supportive of students but could be easily corrected.

Not Ready for Prime Time

- There is no technical information associated with the rubric.
- There have been no studies on the rubric to show that it assesses what is intended.
- The language used in the rubric is not appropriate for the diversity of students found in typical classrooms. The language might include stereotypes, appeal to some learning styles over others, and might put ELL students at a disadvantage. These problems are not easily corrected.
- The language used in the rubric might be hurtful to students. For example, at the low end of the rating scale terms such as "clueless" or "has no idea how to proceed" are used. These problems would not be easy to correct.

Figure 4.1. Continued

Here's the interesting part—the metarubric has to adhere to its own standards of quality. Thus, just as we are asking all rubrics to have good content, to be clear, to be practical, and to be technically sound, our metarubric must also have these features. So, as we proceed through this chapter, see if we've managed to adhere to our own standards.

Any good rubric provides a rationale for the way it is structured. Here's ours:

1. **The descriptors under each trait are not meant as a checklist.** It is not the case that only the things listed under each level have to be present, and if each thing is checked off then the rubric moves to a higher level. Rather, the descriptors under each level are meant as indicators that help the user focus on the important qualities of the performance level (i.e., the correct score). Not all the indicators have to be present—it depends on the way the rubric will be used. The score scale in the metarubric should be seen as describing the sorts of things that are true of rubrics of various levels of quality. See which set of descriptors comes closest to describing the rubric you are evaluating.

2. An odd number of points is used because **the middle score represents a balance of strengths and weaknesses**—the rubric is strong in some ways but weak in others.

3. **A strong score doesn't necessarily mean that the rubric is perfect;** rather, it means that you'd have very little work to do to get it ready for your own use. A weak score means that the rubric needs so much work that it probably isn't worth the effort—it's time to find another one. It might even be easier to begin from scratch. A middle score means that the rubric is about halfway there—it will take some work to make it usable, but it probably is worth the effort.

4. **A middle score does not mean "average."** This is a criterion-referenced scale, not a norm-referenced one. It is meant to describe ideal levels of quality in a rubric, not to describe what is currently available. It could be that the "average" rubric *currently available* is closer to a "not ready for prime time" rating than it is to an "on its way" one.

The scale could easily be expanded to a 5-point scale. In this case, think of "4" as a balance of characteristics from the "5" and "3" levels. Likewise, a "2" would be a balance of characteristics from the "3" and "1" levels.

No performance standard has been set on the metarubric. In other words, there is no "cut" score that indicates when a rubric is "good enough." This determination is left to the user(s).

We're going to examine each of the four traits of the metarubric one by one. For each trait, we provide a definition and show examples of rubrics that are strong, middle-range, and weak. (*Note:* Any sound rubric will go through traits one by one providing a definition and examples of strong, middle, and weak performance on each trait.)

For the weak examples, we've masked the rubrics in some manner to protect the identity of their authors. We've done this because we don't want to embarrass anyone. We're all learning about this together, and authors are allowed to make mistakes. In fact, without these mistakes we'd never know what doesn't work. So, the weak examples are not meant as indictments. We stand on the shoulders of others.

Metarubric Trait 1: Content/Coverage

The content of a rubric defines what to look for in a student's product or performance to determine its quality. Rubric content truly is the final definition of content standards because the rubric describes what will "count." Regardless of what is stated in content standards, curriculum frameworks, or instructional materials, the content of the rubric is what teachers and students will use to determine what they need to do in order to succeed—what they see is what you'll get. Therefore, it is essential that the rubric cover all essential aspects that define quality in a product or performance and leave out all things trivial.

If a rubric contains things other than those that really distinguish quality, teachers won't buy into them, students will not learn what really contributes to quality, and you might find yourself giving ratings to work that you feel in your heart are too high or too low. So, when evaluating a rubric for content, ask yourself these questions:

- Can I explain why each element I have included in my rubric is essential to a quality performance?

- Can I cite references that describe the best thinking in the field on the nature of quality performance?

- Can I describe what I left out, and why I left it out?

- Do I ever find performances or products that are scored low (or high) that I really think are good (or bad)? If so, my rubric needs to be fine-tuned to cover that which is really important.

- Is anything in the rubric not worth the time devoted to it?

Box 4.1 tells stories of times when the content of a rubric was counterproductive to learning. Have you ever experienced situations similar to these?

Next are some examples of rubrics that illustrate different levels of quality on the trait of content/coverage.

> **BOX 4.1**   Vignettes: The Importance of Good Content in a Rubric
>
> **The Two-Minute Oral Presentation**
>
> The son of a colleague was involved in a month-long project that involved researching a topic, writing a research report, and making an oral presentation. The oral presentations were to be between 2 and 3 minutes in length. The son practiced at home and timed his speech at about 2 minutes and 15 seconds. When he gave his oral presentation at school he was a little nervous and spoke faster. His presentation was logged in at 3 seconds under 2 minutes. He was docked two grades for length, from an A to a C.
>
> The point? It might be desirable to have a 2-minute speech, but is this really what is most important in an oral presentation? What message does this send to the students? If length really *is* important, maybe this could be handled by a checklist (✓ = right length). Then use more important criteria to give feedback on quality.
>
> --
>
> **Leaving Out Important Aspects of Writing**
>
> Some state-level writing assessments leave Voice and Word Choice out of their criteria for scoring writing. Their rationale is understandable—they feel that raters couldn't be consistent in their judgment of voice or word choice.
>
> Here's the problem: What impact do you suppose this omission has had on writing instruction in these states? The point is clear: What we assess signals what we value. What we judge with a rubric is what gets taught. Therefore, rubric content needs to reflect what we *really value* when judging quality. What they see is what you'll get.

"Not Ready for Prime Time" on the Metarubric Trait of Content/ Coverage = Informal Writing Assessment *(see Figure 4.2)*

This rubric covers almost nothing that denotes good-quality writing. It is based totally on grammar. What about ideas, organization, voice, word choice, and sentence fluency?

"Not Ready for Prime Time" on the Metarubric Trait of Content/Coverage = Research Report *(see Figure 4.3)*

Here are our initial questions (the reader might think of others):

- Why does it have to be a five-paragraph theme? What if the student has another way to present the information that better makes the points? Isn't the goal to have an organization that fits the message and en-

The Informal Writing Assessment asks young students to respond to a picture—what is happening in the picture, what preceded the picture, what will happen next, and so forth. To score the essay, the rater first counts up the total number of grammatical errors. Then the rater counts up the number of "fatal" grammatical errors—those that are so confusing that meaning is lost. The number of fatal errors is divided by the total number of errors to get the error index. An error index greater than 75% indicates the need for remediation.

Figure 4.2. Informal Writing Assessment Rubric

Students are asked to write a research report on the original 13 colonies. To get an "A," students must do the following:
- Answer all the questions for each colonial region—Where were the colonies located? Who settled each region of colonization? Why did people come to each region? How did people live in each region?

- Use a five-paragraph theme format (introduction, three paragraphs for the body, and a conclusion).

- Have readable cursive writing.

Figure 4.3. Research Report Rubric

   hances the information presented? Sometimes, this might be a five-paragraph theme, but other times, it might not. (Now, if it's clear to students that they are just practicing this one format for writing and that, in general, this is only one way to write, it might be OK.)

- Why is readable cursive writing required? Why not word processing? Why not just have "readability" be a checklist and then go on to rate that which is really important?

- What is the point of writing the report to begin with? What knowledge, skills, and reasoning are the students practicing? This rubric is very heavily loaded on knowledge. Is that worth the time devoted to it? What is this rubric communicating to students about that which is important in a research report?

"Not Ready for Prime Time" on the Metarubric Trait of Content/Coverage = Quantity Descriptors

Consider the rubric that is shown in Figure 4.4.

The students are asked to compare two original sources of information and answer a compare/contrast question. One part of the rubric gives the students points for the amount of information students use in their essay that is not included in the documents. In other words, some students know more historical facts about the topic than others. Here's the rubric:

Prior Knowledge: Facts and Events

0 = no response

1 = no facts/events mentioned that are not found in the text of the debates

2 = one to two pieces of information that are not found in the text of the debates

3 = three to four pieces of information that are not found in the text of the debates

4 = five to six pieces of information that are not found in the text of the debates

5 = seven or more pieces of information that are not found in the text of the debates

Figure 4.4. Quantity Descriptors Rubric

Have you ever had a meal at a restaurant where the portions were gigantic, but the quality was poor? That's the essence with this example—quantity does not always imply quality.

The questions we have about the rubric in Figure 4.4 are these:

- Let's say that Student 1 includes 2 pieces of information that are very insightful, but Student 2 includes 10 pieces of information that have marginal relevance. Student 2 would score higher than Student 1. Shouldn't a couple of really relevant pieces of additional information be worth more than lots of additional information that is marginal or confusing?

- Why assign the given point values to the given numbers of pieces of information to begin with? It looks so arbitrary (see Box 4.2).

"On Its Way" on the Metarubric Trait of Content/Coverage = Oral Presentation Rubric

Before reading on, take a moment to look at the rubric in Figure 4.5 and decide what is left out that might be an important indicator of the quality of an oral presentation. Use the metarubric trait of content/clarity in Figure 4.1 and find the descriptors that describe the *Oral Presentation* rubric. Teachers usu-

---

BOX 4.2   Misconception Alert!

Isn't Counting More Objective?

If the goal with rubrics is to make subjective assessment as objective as possible, won't counting the number of times something occurs in a piece of work help?

You've probably seen rubrics that rely on counts. For example, a student might get a "2" in writing conventions if he or she makes 20 or more spelling, grammatical, punctuation, and capitalization mistakes. But, here's the rub: Shouldn't 20 different mistakes be counted differently than the same mistake made 20 times? Shouldn't errors that really impair the readability of the piece count more than errors that don't?

It sometimes might be the case that quantity implies quality, but not always. **Be careful of counts!**

Score	Language	Presentation	Structure
A = 5	Student uses correct grammar and pronunciation. Words are accurate and used well. Student defines unfamiliar vocabulary.	Volume and rate are appropriate for the audience. There are few distractions such as "um" and "ah." The student holds the listener's attention and maintains effective eye contact. Nonverbal behavior adds to the presentation.	The organization enhances the message. The speaker sticks to the topic. It is easy to follow. The opening catches the listener's attention. Pacing is good.
B = 4 C = 3	Student uses correct grammar and pronunciation. Words are adequate and understandable. Student does not define unfamiliar terms. The listener must make some inferences to understand what is meant.	The speaker can be generally heard and understood. The speaker generally maintains eye contact with the audience. Volume and rate of presentation are somewhat appropriate for the audience.	The organization is workable. There is a recognizable introduction and conclusion. The speaker may shift unexpectedly from one point to another, or pacing might be off. The speech can be summarized.
D = 2 F = 1	There are many errors in grammar and pronunciation. Words are used incorrectly or are not effective. The listener must make many inferences to understand what is meant.	The student's volume and rate is not appropriate for the audience. There may be frequent pauses and use of many "ums" and "ahs." Nonverbal behaviors tend to interfere with the message.	The presentation lacks a clear sense of direction. The relationships between ideas are not clear. Ideas, details, or events seem strung together in a random fashion. It is hard to summarize the speech.

Figure 4.5. Oral Presentation Rubric

ally find that this rubric covers many valued elements in an oral presentation but leaves out a couple of very important things—for example, the quality of the *content* of the presentation. Teachers also tend to want to refine the indicators for the traits of delivery and language.

"On Its Way" on the Metarubric Trait of Content/Coverage = Writing Rubrics That Leave Out Voice and/or Word Choice

These rubrics have much to like; they just need to be fine-tuned.

"On Its Way" on the Metrarubric Trait of Content/Coverage = Business Letter Rubric

Before reading on, take a look at Figure 4.6. Compare this rubric to the metarubric trait of content/coverage. What words and phrases do you find in the metarubric that describe the *Business Letter* rubric?

The criteria listed in the rubric are a good start but could use work. The list of things to be evaluated is a little daunting—it sprawls. Since many of the listed indicators seem to go together, they might profitably be grouped into five general categories, or "traits." By attempting to group them into traits, it also becomes clear what is left out of the rubric.

1. **Content.** Does the letter cover what it needs to cover? Is the information accurate? Has the applicant does his or her homework? Does the letter cover the skills needed for the job? This trait would include Items 10–14 of the rubric in Figure 4.6.

2. **Voice/Style/Flair/Penetrability.** Is the letter written in such a way that the interviewer wants to read it? Does it have a professional, earnest, sincere voice? This trait would include Item 20 of the rubric (but more would need to be added to really fill out this trait).

3. **Organization.** Is the letter organized well? Currently, there are no items in the developer's criteria that relate to organization.

4. **Format/Presentation.** Is this, in fact, a job application letter? Does it have the proper format, opening, and so forth? This trait would include Items 1–9, 15–19, and 22 of the rubric. In fact, the criteria, as listed, are weighted very heavily on format. Is this the emphasis desired? Is this the message that should be sent to students?

5. **Mechanics/Conventions.** Is the letter free of spelling and grammar errors? This would include Item 21 of the rubric. But some mechanics and conventions are left out. Might there also be other conventions to look for, such as paragraphing, capitalization, and punctuation?

Each of the following is to be rated on a scale from 1 to 3.

1. The letter opens with the addressee's name

2. Title of addressee

3. Name of company

4. Address, city, state

5. ZIP code

6. This is followed by a double space

7. The salutation includes addressee's name

8. This is followed by a ":"

9. This is followed by a double space

10. The letter opens with a strong, positive statement about the applicant or his qualifications or opens with a statement naming a person known by the addressee who advised the applicant of available position

11. The letter highlights the best items from applicant's background which directly qualifies him for the job

12. The letter states why the applicant wants to work for this organization

13. The letter requests an interview

14. The letter suggests how the applicant will follow up or where he can be reached to schedule an interview

15. The letter includes a proper closing followed by a comma

16. The closing is followed by four hard returns

17. The applicant's full real name is typed below the closing

18. The applicant signs the letter in ink between the closing and his name

19. The letter is one page

20. Sentences and paragraphs are short and easy to read

21. There are no misspelled words or grammar errors

22. The letter is printed on high-quality paper

Figure 4.6. Business Letter Rubric
SOURCE: Adapted from a rubric developed by Anna Lipski, Grossmont High School, La Mesa, CA.

The other major problem with this rubric is that, as written, Item 10 might be limiting and might result in some good letters being called "bad." The criteria only allow two possible openings for the letter. What if neither of these is appropriate for the particular job being applied for? Or what happens if the student comes up with a very catchy, yet highly appropriate, way to begin?

Thus, the trait of "content" might need to be reworked to really describe what is meant by a quality opening.[1]

"Ready to Roll" on the Metrarubric Trait of Content/Coverage = Six-Trait + 1 Model
(see Figure 2.2 and the Resource section)

Teachers tend to see this rubric as really defining the nature of quality writing. It has been embraced and used nationwide to teach and assess writing in the classroom.

This doesn't, however, mean that it is perfect. Every good rubric is constantly under development to continue to home in on just that which most distinguishes quality. For example, the trait of "sentence fluency" began its life as "sentence correctness." Teachers began having questions about this trait when they encountered sentence fragments that worked very well (in fact, were crafted by the author) to create a feeling in a piece of writing. A sentence fragment is not a complete sentence, and so the student's work had to be scored low on the trait of sentence correctness.

The solution? (Please note the sentence fragment.) Modify the trait of "sentence correctness" to "sentence fluency." What we're really looking for is that *students are in control* of sentence structure—they can use complete sentences when they are needed, or they can intentionally use fragments when they add to the feel of the piece. Box 4.3 summarizes this common pitfall.

Bottom Line on the Metarubric Trait of Content/Coverage

Look through the rubric. Does it cover that which is essential? Does it leave out that which isn't essential? Does it send the right message to students about what is important? Could you buy into this rubric?

A rubric that does not cover the essential aspects of a performance will not be used and is not useful.

 ## Metarubric Trait 2: Clarity/Detail

The more detail the better. A rubric is clear to the extent that teachers, students, and others are likely to interpret the statements and terms in the rubric the same way. Please notice that a rubric can be strong on the trait of content/coverage but weak on the trait of clarity—the rubric seems to cover the important dimensions of performance, but they aren't described very well. Likewise, a rubric can be strong on the trait of clarity but weak on the trait of content/ coverage—it's very clear what the rubric means, it's just not very important stuff.

Questions to ask yourself when evaluating a rubric for clarity are these:

- Would two teachers be likely to give the same rating on a product or performance?
- Could I find examples of student work or performances that illustrate each level of quality?

Have samples of student work to illustrate what you mean. Ask yourself, "Could I show someone else samples of student work or performances that specifically illustrate each score point on each dimension?"

Here are some sample rubrics that illustrate different levels of clarity on the metarubric.

"Not Ready for Prime Time" on the Metarubric Trait of Clarity = Skimpy Criteria Rubric *(see Figure 4.7)*

Look at the metarubric trait of clarity/detail in Figure 4.1. Find the words that describe the *Skimpy Criteria* rubric in Figure 4.7.

Here are the words we found: The language is very vague. There are no definitions. The rubric is nothing more than a list of categories to rate followed by a rating scale. There are no descriptors given to define the levels of performance. Teachers would probably be very unlikely to agree on scores.

	Frequently	Occasionally	Sometimes	Never
Understanding the problem	4	3	2	1
Correct use of math	4	3	2	1
Good strategies and reasoning	4	3	2	1
Effective communication	4	3	2	1

Figure 4.7. Skimpy Criteria Rubric

"Not Ready for Prime Time" on the Metarubric Trait of Clarity = Rubric for Small Group Discussion (see Figure 4.8)

Once again consult the metarubric (see Figure 4.1) on the trait of clarity/ detail. What words do you find that describe the rubric in Figure 4.8?

First, there are some content issues here that relate to the first trait in the metarubric. Does this rubric really cover everything of most importance? Does it sprawl? Might it benefit from having similar items grouped to form traits?

But, regardless of the content issues, there are also issues of clarity. Would raters agree on, for example, when something is loud enough to be heard easily? Does the introduction of any new idea count, or just relevant ideas? The items in the list lack clarity, and there are no descriptors for various levels. Everyone is left just to guess.

This is an example of an attempt to use a checklist or an assessment list when a rubric is needed instead.

Rate each of the following with a ✓–, ✓ or, ✓+.

1. Speaks loudly and clearly enough to be heard easily.

2. Introduces new ideas.

3. Uses reasoning and evidence to support new ideas.

4. Asks questions to get information.

5. Summarizes when needed.

6. Tries to include others in the discussion.

7. Disagrees tactfully.

8. Listens to and follows the flow of conversation.

Figure 4.8. Rubric for Small Group Discussion

1 point: Shows no understanding of the requirements of the problem.

2 points: Shows a little understanding of the requirements of the problem.

3 points: Shows partial understanding of the requirements of the problem.

4 points: Shows considerable understanding of the requirements of the problem.

5 points: Shows complete understanding of the requirements of the problem.

Figure 4.9. Rubric for Problem Solving

"Not Ready for Prime Time" on the Metarubric Trait of Clarity = Rubric for Problem Solving *(see Figure 4.9)*

How many rubrics have you seen that are no more than this? In this example, the only thing that distinguishes the levels are very general and vague statements like "no understanding, some understanding, and considerable understanding."

We would like to propose to the reader that it is rubrics like these that lead to criticisms of performance assessment by teachers, students, parents, and the press. In fact, we recently saw an editorial in a local newspaper that ridiculed performance assessment and cited examples like the above to bolster their case. If we want our performance assessments to have credibility, they need to be much less subjective. It is the descriptive detail that results in clear definitions and consistent scoring that give rubrics credibility.

"On Its Way" on the Metarubric Trait of Clarity = Oral Presentation Rubric *(see Figure 4.5)*

Look at the metarubric trait of clarity/detail in Figure 4.1 and find the language that describes this rubric.

Clearly, this rubric has more detail and clarity than those above. Here are the words from the metarubric that seem to describe this rubric. "There is some attempt to define terms and include descriptors, but it doesn't go far enough." Specifically, what is the difference between a "4" and a "3" in the middle category and between a "2" and a "1" in the lower category? There is no attempt to define the major headings, although there is an attempt to define levels. Teachers would agree on how to rate some things in the rubric while others are not well-enough defined.

(Note: We have included the level descriptions just for the first trait. The other traits have similar level descriptions.)

A. I find meaning in information and then combine and organize information to make it useful for my task.

    4   I find useful and accurate meaning in information I gather for my task. I understand meanings in information that other people do not see. I then combine and organize information in my own way to express certain ideas.

    3   I find useful and accurate meaning in the information I gather for my task, and I combine and organize the information so that it makes sense.

    2   I make errors when I look for meaning in information that I gather for my task, and I combine the information inaccurately or in a way that makes it confusing.

    1   I make major errors when I look for meaning in information that I gather for my task, and I do not combine or organize information.

B. I use a variety of methods and resources when gathering information for my task.

C. I accurately determine how valuable specific information may be to my task.

D. I recognize when more information is needed and explain how the new information would improve the completed project.

Figure 4.10. Rubric for Research/Information Processing
SOURCE: © 1993 McREL. Used with permission.

"On Its Way" on the Metarubric Trait of Clarity = Rubric for Research/Information Processing (see Figure 4.10)

What are the words in the metarubric trait of clarity (Figure 4.1) that describe this rubric in Figure 4.10?
This rubric attempts to define levels, but it doesn't go far enough.

"Ready to Roll" on the Metarubric Trait of Clarity = Six-Trait + 1 Model (see Figure 2.2 and Resource)

Terms are defined. Words are specific and accurate. Levels are defined with lots of descriptive detail, and scored samples are readily available. There is an abundance of evidence that teachers (and students) can learn to score writing consistently.

Task: The students are given a picture of a stack of cubes (not all of which can be seen). They are asked: (a) How many cubes are needed to build this tower? (b) How many cubes are needed to build a tower like this, but 12 cubes high? Explain how you worked out this answer. (c) How would you calculate the number of cubes needed for a tower "n" cubes high?

Rubric:

4 = Three correct answers with strategies shown.

    a. Each side has 15 blocks. $15 \times 4 = 60$. There are 6 blocks in the center column. $60 + 6 = 66$.

    b. Each side: $11 + 10 + 9 + 8 + 7 + 6 + 5 + 4 + 3 + 2 + 1 = 66$. Four sides: $66 \times 4 = 264$ plus center column: $264 + 12 = 276$ blocks.

    c. Total number of blocks $= n = 4$ (sum from 1 to infinity of $n-1$).

3 = Response shows either two correct answers with support, with or without attempt to solve other parts, or three correct answers with little or no strategy shown.

2 = Response shows either one answer with support and attempts other part(s), or two correct answers with no support.

1 = Response is off-task with irrelevant answer(s) or shows one correct answer with no support, or no attempt to solve other two parts, or three parts are attempted with no conceptual understanding demonstrated.

0 = Blank.

Figure 4.11. KIRIS Grade 12 Mathematics Rubric

SOURCE: Used with permission of the Kentucky Department of Education, Frankfort, Kentucky, 40601.

"Ready to Roll" on the Metarubric Trait of Clarity = KIRIS Grade 12 Mathematics Rubric *(see Figure 4.11)*

This is a task-specific rubric but is very detailed on what, specifically, constitutes a correct answer. Several samples of student work are attached to assist scoring. (We didn't include the samples here for brevity's sake.)

Bottom Line on the Metarubric Trait of Clarity

Try scoring samples of student work in your classroom using these various rubrics and you'll see why clarity is important—it helps you be consistent across students, over time, and across teachers.

Shouldn't It Fit on One Page?

Beware the person who says, "To be useful the rubric has to fit on one page." The goal is to be clear, not to be brief at the expense of clarity. Sometimes you can be perfectly clear on one page. Sometimes it takes six pages, as with the Six-Trait Model in Writing. The more complex the skill or product being defined, the more need for detail (and, therefore, length). After all, it's the hardest things to define, like problem solving, critical thinking, and lifelong learning, that *most* need to be defined. It's unlikely that satisfactory clarity for complex skills and products can fit on one page.

But that's not the only point. Additionally, detail helps clearly communicate to students what they need to do to produce quality work. Students have a harder time generating another strong response if they don't know what made the previous response strong. Or if the previous response is weak, they have a harder time making the next one better if they don't know what made the current one weak.

Therefore, purpose is related to design. If the purpose of the criteria is use as an instructional tool in the classroom, then adequate detail is of paramount importance. If the purpose is merely to put numbers on student work for large-scale assessment, perhaps not as much detail is important.

Clarity versus brevity in a rubric's length is discussed in Box 4.4.

Metarubric Trait 3: Usability

Having clear rubrics that cover the right "stuff" means nothing if the system is too cumbersome to use. The trait of practicality refers to ease of use—can teachers and students understand and use it easily? Does it give them the information they need for instructional decision making and tracking student progress toward important learning outcomes? Can the rubric be used for more than just a way to assess students? Can it also be used to improve the very achievement also being assessed?

Questions to ask yourself about a rubric are these:

- Will the results from this rubric show me what I need to do next in instruction?

- Can I define each statement in my rubric in such a way that students can understand what I mean?

- Would I know what to say if a student asks "Why did I get this score?"

- Would these criteria communicate to a student who is not doing well what to do differently next time?

In general, the answers to these questions imply generic, analytical trait rubrics.

Here are some examples of rubrics that illustrate various levels on the metarubric trait of usability.

"Not Ready for Prime Time" on the Metarubric Trait of Usability = Skimpy Criteria Rubric *(see Figure 4.7)*

Look at the metarubric trait of usability in Figure 4.1. Find the words that describe the *Skimpy Criteria* rubric.

The lack of clarity is a major problem for usability here. Although it could give some information to teachers on where to focus instruction, it is unlikely that students would understand the rubric, be able to rate their own work, or know what to do differently next time in order to improve performance. For example, would students know how to improve their work if they got an "occasionally" on "Effective Communication"?

"Not Ready for Prime Time" on the Metarubric Trait of Usability = Quantity Descriptors Rubric *(see Figure 4.4)*

What words in the metarubric trait of usability (see Figure 4.1) describe this rubric? There is no justification given for the type of rubric used—why are counts appropriate? There seems to be no consideration of how the rubric might be useful to teachers. The intent seems to be only large-scale assessment efficiency. It is not clear how to translate results into instruction. How would this rubric help students learn?

"Not Ready for Prime Time" on the Metarubric Trait of Usability = KIRIS Grade 12 Mathematics Rubric *(see Figure 4.11)*

Even though this rubric has enough detail that it would be easy to train raters and get consistent scoring, it appears to lack usefulness in the classroom. There is no justification for the type of rubric used. Again, the goal appears to be large-scale efficiency. There seems to be no consideration of how the rubric might be useful to teachers. The rubric is manageable, but it is not clear how to translate the results into instruction. What if your classroom averaged a 3.2? How might you alter instruction? How would students use this rubric to improve achievement?

In fact, is it clear at all what is being assessed by this rubric? Is it some sort of mathematical knowledge? Is it problem solving? Is it communication in mathematics? Perhaps a generic, analytical trait rubric would be better for use in the classroom.

"On Its Way" on the Metarubric Trait of Usability = Business Letter Rubric *(see Figure 4.6)*

Look at the metarubric trait of usability in Figure 4.1. Find the words that describe the *Business Letter* rubric.

We've had many teachers tell us that the original list is just too long—it would take forever to rate everybody on all those features. Thus, the rubric provides some useful information but is not easy to use. Recombining the rubric into traits, as we did above, helps.

Even though the developer has not done so, it is easy to see how the assessment can be used to enhance students' achievement through their involvement:

1. You could ask students to "re-create" (or add to) the criteria for quality by looking at previous samples of student job applications and video clips of interviews.

2. One could ask students to critique the job applications or video clip interviews of other students.

3. One could ask students to practice, with feedback from the teacher and their peers.

4. One could ask students to keep track of their performance over time and analyze how first attempts are different from current attempts.

5. Students could report the analysis in Item 4 to others.

These procedures would help students see and understand the intended achievement targets, practice hitting the targets, and self-assess. They would probably also help the students be more confident in the job interview and knowledgeably discuss the criteria by which they will be judged.

The rubric thus has potential for student self-use but needs some tweaking—streamlining and making the format more appealing.

"Ready to Roll" on the Metarubric Trait of Usability = Six-Trait Model *(see Figure 2.2 and Resource)*

Look at the metarubric trait of usability in Figure 4.1. Find the words that describe the *Six-Trait Model.*

For the Six-Trait Model, the intended use is instructional; therefore, the rubric is both generic and analytical trait. It takes a while to learn the rubric, but there is unanimous consensus across the country that the instructional payoff is worth the time. It is clear how to translate results into instruction. There are student-friendly versions available for primary, elementary, and secondary students. (One student-friendly version is included in the Resource section.) There are lots of support material available to help teachers help students use these criteria to be self-assessors and revisers of their own writing. (These sources are also given in the Resource section.)

"Ready to Roll" on the Metarubric Trait of Usability = Central Kitsap Mathematics Rubric *(see Resource)*

Once again, the rubric is analytical trait (four traits) and generic—it can be used to profile strengths and weaknesses and can be used across mathematics problems. There are student-friendly versions available—the example in the Resource section is a student-friendly version. It provides instructional information.

Bottom Line on the Metarubric Trait of Usability

In this book, our emphasis is on the classroom. Therefore, our recommendations for rubrics—analytical trait and generic—are heavily influenced by this choice.

Metarubric Trait 4: Technical Quality

It is important to have "hard" evidence that a rubric adequately measures the skills being assessed, that it can be applied consistently, and that there is reason to believe that the ratings actually do represent what students can do. Although this might be beyond the scope of what individual classroom teachers can do, we all still have the responsibility to ask hard questions when we adopt or develop a rubric. A big factor in these considerations is fairness—will the rubric place any group at a disadvantage solely because of the way the rubric is worded, and not because of skill level?

The following rubrics illustrate various levels of quality on the metarubric trait of technical quality.

"Not Ready for Prime Time" on the Metarubric Trait
of Technical Quality = Skimpy Criteria Rubric *(see Figure 4.7)*

This rubric was used to score student responses to a state assessment. Teachers were asked to rate student mathematics problems without training. Rater agreement rates were very low—around 33%. This is evidence that, as used, the rubric was not technically sound.

"On Its Way" on the Metarubric Trait of Technical
Quality = Six-Trait Model *(see Figure 2.2 and Resource)*

Experienced raters reach exact agreement rates between 65% and 75%. Raters are within one point more than 98% of the time. This is evidence that, as used, the rubric is technically sound.

There is a Spanish version of the rubric—students still write in English, but the rubric is in Spanish. The goal is that ELL students don't have an extra burden of understanding the rubric.

Balancing the very positive technical information and the accommodations for ELL students is the fact that the wording in the rubric is a little negative at the lower end. This is what keeps the Six-Trait Model from being strong on the metarubric trait of technical quality. This is true of many of the rubrics in the Resource section. Take a look and see if you can identify such wording.

"On Its Way" on the Metarubric Trait of Technical
Quality = Central Kitsap Mathematics Rubric *(see Resource)*

Look at the metarubric trait of technical quality in Figure 4.1. Find the words that describe the *Central Kitsap Mathematics* rubric.

The wording is very supportive of students—the wording states what the student did or did not do (and what the student may or may not be thinking) rather than a judgment of the worth of the work. Additionally, the rubric has been reviewed by several groups for bias in wording. The problem with this rubric is that there is no technical information. Therefore, on the metarubric trait of technical quality, the Central Kitsap Mathematics rubric shows a balance of strengths and weaknesses and so is in the middle.

"On Its Way" on the Metarubric Trait of Technical Quality = Juneau Primary Reading Continuum Rubric *(see Resource)*

This rubric is strong in the area of positive wording. The wording at all the levels of the continuum is very descriptive. It's not that one level is innately superior to another; rather, they are merely stages of development through which all students pass. But, once again, there is no technical information to show that raters (and students) can be consistent in their scoring. Since the rubric shows a balance of strengths and weaknesses on the metarubric trait of technical quality, it would get a middle rating.

Please notice that we have not cited any "high" examples. We haven't found any yet that combine all the features of a strong rubric on this trait—technical information, fairness, and positive wording.

Bottom Line on the Metarubric Trait of Technical Quality

If students never see the rubric, then you can use any language you want. If, however, the goal is instructional and students are expected to understand and apply the rubric, then wording is everything. Once again, purpose and use dictate rubric design.

Conducting technical studies on the rubrics you use is also informative. If you can achieve high rater-agreement rates—even in your own classroom among your own students, you've got a credible rubric.

Chapter Summary

This chapter presented a rubric for quality rubrics—a metarubric. This metarubric has four traits—shown in Box 4.5. The metarubric is itself a rubric. Therefore, it has to adhere to its own standards. So, we attempted to model the very features described in the metarubric. We (a) described the major dimensions (traits) that define quality on rubrics; (b) defined each metarubric trait and showed high, medium, and low examples of each; and (c) tried to make the metarubric practical. We didn't, however, model "technical soundness." We have no data that show that raters can consistently rate the quality of rubrics the same using the metarubric.

BOX 4.5   Characteristics of High-Quality Rubrics

1. **Content/Coverage**—Does the rubric cover the features that really indicate quality performance?
2. **Clarity/Detail**—Does the rubric make it clear what you mean with definitions, indicators, and samples of work?
3. **Practicality**—Do teachers and students find it useful for instruction and assessment?
4. **Technical Quality/Soundness/Fairness**—Can you get raters to agree on scores? Is the rubric fair to all students?

Note

1. This analysis was done by Judy apart from this book and used with permission of the Assessment Training Institute.

CHAPTER 5

Performance Standards and Grading

Guiding Question: How good is "good enough?"

We used to think that developing rubrics was where the rubber met the road. We've changed our minds. Developing rubrics is certainly important—they define what we mean by quality. But rubrics are not truly complete until we decide on the "performance standard"—the level of performance on the rubric that we'll call "meeting standard" or "being competent."

Setting "performance standards" is a cornerstone of standards-based education. For example, say you have a 6-point scale for assessing mathematics (like the California example in Figure 2.1 and the Resource section). Well, how good does performance have to be on this rubric at Grade 3, Grade 6, Grade 8, and Grade 11 in order for us to feel that students are either progressing adequately toward competency on the standard (Grades 3, 6, and 8) or have met the standard (Grade 10 or 11)? Is it a 3? A 4? A 5?

Setting performance standards on rubrics is not taking place just on district, state, and national assessments. The classroom parallel to setting performance standards is grading (see Box 5.1). What level of performance earns an "A" in your classroom? How do you decide where on the rubric a "C" should be? In both large-scale assessments and the classroom, the same question must be answered—how good is good enough?

In this chapter, we outline several methods used in large-scale assessments for setting the "official" performance standards on rubrics. These methods are applicable to the

> **BOX 5.1   Misconception Alert!**
>
> Setting performance standards on a rubric doesn't only occur at the large-scale state and national levels. The classroom equivalent is grading—how do you convert rubric scores to grades? How good is good enough to get an "A"? A "B"? An "F"?

Table 5.1 Example of a Predefined Performance Standard

Score	Point Definition
4	The performance exceeds expectations for the grade level.
3	The performance meets expectations for the grade level.
2	The performance indicates an attempt was made but does not meet the expectations for the grade level.
1	The performance partially meets expectations for the grade level.
0	No attempt was made (or the response was unscorable).

school and classroom as well. Then, we look at some suggestions for using rubrics in grading.

Setting Performance Standards

Choice 1 for Setting Standards on Large-Scale Assessments—Afterward or Before

Afterward: Develop the rubric first and then go back and decide how good is "good enough." This method was used in Oregon to set performance standards in reading, writing, and mathematics. (The reading rubric is in the Resource section.) Oregon used generic analytical trait scoring guides for years before having to set performance standards on them. Therefore, they had to go back and establish the performance standards after the rubrics were developed.

Oregon set their standards by asking groups of educators (and the public) to sort student work into two groups at each "benchmark" grade level—work that was "good enough" for that grade and work that was "not good enough" for that grade. Then they went back and determined what scores the papers in the two stacks typically receive. In writing, "meets competency" falls at a score point of "3" or "4" (on a scale of 1 to 6) depending on grade level and trait. (Note: Since Oregon uses an analytical trait system, they set performance standards trait by trait.)

Before: Decide ahead of time the numerical value you want as the "performance standard" and then define that number to reflect the characteristics of a "competent" performance. This is the approach taken by NWREL Mathematics (see Resource). A typical approach for setting the performance standard by Method 2 is shown in Table 5.1. Notice how the score points are predefined.

In this example, these criteria are very skimpy—much more detail is needed on the specific features (either general or task-specific) to indicate when the various levels have been obtained.

Here's how the method plays out. First, a large group of experienced educators and others get together and sort work into five groups or stacks—exceeds expectations, meets expectations, almost (or partially) meets expectations, does not meet expectations, and no attempt. Second, each stack is reviewed to determine the distinguishing characteristics of the responses in that stack. These distinguishing characteristics become the rubric descriptors for that level. So, the rubric descriptors for a "3" automatically define the "meets expectations" level.

So, how do you decide which approach to use? Consider the following:

- *How many scale points will meet your needs?* Four points may not be enough for instructional uses; you might want to make finer distinctions. For example, you might want your students to be able to steadily see gains as measured against a rubric. This argues for a 5- or 6-point scale. But if the primary use for the rubric is certifying competence, then a 4-point scale might be sufficient. Of course, you could always have a 5- or 6-point scale, where "4" is automatically defined as "meets expectation." This would give more score points, while still allowing you to predefine your levels.

- *How many "performance standards" do you want to set?* On analytical trait rubrics, you have to set a performance standard on each trait. This might not be worth the effort if all one is going to do with the rubric is certify student competence. If, however, the rubric and standards are to be used in the classroom for instruction, the additional detail and information might be very useful. For example, in writing, it might be useful to know that most of the class have met the standard on the traits of "word choice," "voice," and "conventions" but have not met the standard on the traits of "ideas," "organization," and "sentence fluency." This information helps teachers focus instruction.

- *How confused are users likely to become?* Developing rubrics first and then setting performance standards can lead to different scores on different traits that "meet the standard." Some folks like to have the same score on each trait (and rubric) signify competence, just so that it's easier to remember. In Oregon, for example, "meets expectation" can be anywhere from a "3" to a "5" (on a scale of 1 to 6) depending on the grade level and trait. This can be confusing to some.

Choice 2 for Setting Performance Standards— Absolute Scales Versus Relative Scales

So far so good. Now here's where it starts getting a little complicated. Consider the following options.

Absolute Scale Approach

We use absolute scales for height, weight, shoe size, temperature, and many other things. Pediatricians track the growth of babies and toddlers to make sure they are growing adequately. There's not a separate scale for each age—the same old inches and feet are used for everyone. Three feet at age 4 is exactly the same height as three feet at age 6. What differs is the "standard" that doctors use for determining when height and weight are OK for various aged children. For example, doctors might call the normal range between two and three feet for children aged 1, between four and five feet for children aged 10, and so on. Children outside these "normal" ranges might cause red flags to be raised.

Now, let's look at the same thing only with an absolute rubric scale. Let's say that you are using an absolute rubric scale of 6 points for writing. A "3" at Grade 4 would mean exactly the same thing as a "3" at Grade 11—the quality of the writing would look the same. To get a "3" in writing at Grade 3, the writing would have to be the same as a "3" in writing at Grade 11. If you mixed up the papers and didn't tell raters which grade was which, the papers would still get the same scores. This is an "absolute scale" because it doesn't matter what grade you're in—a "3" is a "3" is a "3."

Then you'd designate the "performance standard" by saying how far along this "developmental continuum" you'd like students to be by the time they reach various grade levels. For example, you might say that adequate progress for students at Grade 3 would be a score of "2"; at Grade 5, students need to be at "3," at Grade 8 to be up to "4," and at Grade 11 to hit the final goal—at least a "5." Students whose performance is lower than the designated score at a "benchmark" grade might raise a red flag.

For example, look at the *Wauwatosa* writing continuum in the Resource section. A piece of writing that scores a "4" at Grade 1 has exactly the same features as one that scores a "4" at Grade 5. Grade level is not taken into account. Teachers in any grade level from 1 to 5 can track progress continuously.

Now for setting the performance standard. The *Wauwatosa* example specifically says that, by the end of Grade 2, students should have entered Step 8. By the end of the fifth grade, many students will be at Step 10. This could be seen as the performance standard—we want students to be at Step 8 by Grade 2 and at Step 10 by Grade 5.

Absolute scales work well for developmental continuums that have lots of score points.

Relative Scale Approach

You could instead use the same rubric at each grade level but let the samples of student work that illustrate the various score points vary. In this case, a "4" at Grade 3 looks different from a "4" at Grade 11. To get a "4" at Grade 11, the work would have to be better. The score a paper would get is relative to the grade level—a piece of work that you might consider good if produced by a third grader, you might consider fairly weak if produced by a tenth grader.

For example, consider the state of Oregon. The same rubric is used in Grades 3–12 for reading, writing, oral communication, group work, and so forth. What changes are the anchor performances used to illustrate the score points at each grade level. In Oregon, a "competent" performance might always be a "4," but a "4" at Grade 3 looks different from a "4" at Grade 11. Oregon and lots of other places use this approach because teachers tend to like it. They like having lots of score points to use at each grade level, while still taking grade level into account.

Setting Performance Standards—The Bottom Line

Setting a performance standard—a cut-off at which performance is called competent—boils down to (a) before or afterward, (b) number of score points, and (c) absolute or relative. Those are the choices, and they are mix and match. You can have an absolute 11-point scale in which the performance standards were set for each grade level after the fact. Or you can have a 6-point absolute scale where the performance standards were set beforehand.

We recommend a broad range of score points and an absolute scale for developmental continuums because it makes so much sense to track progress continuously over time. This is especially true in the lower grade levels in areas like reading and writing. Then the performance standard might be set after or before the fact.

But we also like absolute scales. These work well when you're going to restrict yourself to 4-point ratings and call "3" competent.

Grading

And now we come to the issue raised in every discussion about rubrics—what about grading? To really tackle this issue and offer concrete suggestions about converting rubric scores to grades, we need to come to grips with some fundamental issues about grading, rubrics, and the relationship between the two.

What does a letter grade (A, B, etc.) represent? What should go into a grade? Do you agree that a grade should represent only level of achievement? Or should we also include motivation, trying hard, getting work in on time, finishing all the homework, and all the other things that sometimes get factored in?

What does a score on a rubric represent? A rubric score indicates only achievement. It is a symbolic representation of a performance level, which is defined by the descriptors for that level.

How are these related? If we agree that grades should primarily communicate achievement and that a grade should include only information about achievement, then grades and rubric scores are indeed very closely related. If we don't agree that grades should only reflect achievement and be used to communicate, then we'll have trouble factoring rubric scores into grades.

Assuming that we agree that grades should primarily communicate about achievement and that a grade should include only information about achievement, quality rubrics that truly describe progress could replace grades. Rubrics that have rich descriptors of various levels of achievement illustrated with actual samples of student work would communicate achievement even better than a grade.

As a practical matter, however, we don't believe that will happen any time soon. Grades are too engrained in our system of education. Also, let's face it, we're not good enough yet at using rubrics and other alternative forms of communicating about achievement to toss out grades. We shouldn't eliminate grades until we're sure we have something better (understood and embraced by all) to replace them. If you want a public relations nightmare, try replacing grades with rubrics or student-led parent conferences before all teachers are adept at using these things.

So, given that we'll likely be using grades for awhile, here's our best advice about how to proceed in generating letter grades from rubrics. (Box 5.2 states what *not* to do.)

Let's assume that a student has received the following rubric scores, shown in Table 5.2, on eight written assignments using the Six-Trait Model.

Looking at Agatha's pattern of scores, what grade do you think she earned? How did you determine this grade? What considerations do you have?

| BOX 5.2 | Misconception Alert! |

The best way to convert a rubric score to a grade is to add up all the points the student earned and divide by the total number of points possible. This percentage can be directly converted to a grade using standard percentage conversion systems. Wrong!

The tempting thing to do is to add up all the points (in this case, 165) and divide by the number of points possible (in this case, 8 papers × 6 scores × 5 points = 240). This would result in 69%. What grade would that be in your school district? C? D?

What do you see that's wrong with this procedure? We see several things wrong.

1. A "3" when divided by the total number of points possible (5) equals 60%, which, in many places converts to an "F." But look at the rubric descrip-

Table 5.2 Agatha's Six-Trait Scores on Eight Papers

Paper	Ideas	Organization	Voice	Word Choice	Sentence Fluency	Conventions	Total
#1 9/22	2	2	2	2	3	3	14
#2 10/15	3	3	2	2	3	2	15
#3 11/30	3	3	3	3	3	3	18
#4 1/5	4	3	3	3	4	3	20
#5 2/8	3	4	4	4	3	4	22
#6 3/14	4	3	4	3	4	4	22
#7 4/12	5	5	5	4	4	3	26
#8 5/18	5	5	5	5	4	4	28
Total	29	28	28	26	28	26	165

tion for a "3." A "3" doesn't indicate failing work. So it is misleading to add up points and divide by the number possible.

2. Say a student got a "1" on a trait. This would convert to 20%. Maybe a "1" really does denote an "F." But it would take a lot of 4s (80%) to balance out a single "1" if you want the average to go above 60%. Is this fair? Maybe a "1" should convert to 60%, not 20%.

3. Should work done at the end of the grading period count more than work done at the beginning? After all, who cares how well a student writes at the beginning, as long as she writes well at the end? If we just counted the final three papers, the percentage would jump to 76 ÷ 90 = 84%. Even just using total points, this would earn Agatha a "B" (see Box 5.3 for an example of how choice with respect to grading can affect student motivation to try).

So, here's what we recommend.

Don't use strict percentages when translating rubric scores to letter grades. While a percentage model could work just fine for tests and quizzes (e.g., Sharon answered

---

BOX 5.3 The Case of the Disappearing Motivation

What would happen in a classroom of "remedial writers" if the teacher insisted on including the scores on every single paper throughout the whole semester into the final grade?

Would it be better to tell the students at the beginning that (a) all papers will be scored on one or more chosen traits as students are learning about what constitutes good writing but that (b) the final grade depends only on how well students write at the end of the semester?

Table 5.3 Logic Rule for Converting Rubric Scores to Grades

If the student gets:	The grade should be:
No more than 10% of scores lower than a 4, with at least 40% 5s	A
No more than 30% of scores lower than a 4, with at least 10% 5s	B
No more than 10% of scores lower than a 3, with at least 20% 4 or better	C
No more than 30% of scores lower than a 3, with at least 10% 4 or better	D
Anything lower than this	F

80% of the items on a multiple-choice test correctly), they are misleading when converted from rubric scores.

The *preferred method* is to come up with a **logic rule** for deciding on grades. Table 5.3 shows an example.

If this were the grading procedure, what grade would Agatha get? (Now, don't go right out and use this scheme. We just made it up as an example. Come up with one you can live with.)

Second best way to convert rubric scores to grades: Decide from the descriptions in the rubric what grade each score should earn. For example, "4" and "5" might be an "A," "3" might be a "B," and "2" might be a "C." Therefore, all 4s and 5s would convert to whatever percentage you give As, say 90%, 3s would convert to 80%, 2s would convert to 70%, and 1s would convert to 60%. In this case, what grade would Agatha get?

Bottom Line on Grading

Unless teachers completely agree on the elements that should be included in a grade (achievement, motivation, ability, etc.) and factor them into grading in consistent ways, the meaning of grades will vary from classroom to classroom. While there is much more to say on this subject, we'll leave you with the following contention: To make grading more meaningful and consistent, separate grades that describe achievement from grades for other factors, such as progress, effort, work completion, behavior, and so forth. Otherwise, students could earn the same grade for very different reasons. How effective is such a communication system?

And convert rubric scores to grades in ways that make sense—not percentages but logic rules. The grade needs to reflect the actual achievement; how will you ensure that it does? Whatever methods you decide to use, make sure everyone (teachers, students, parents, and the community) understands the scheme and supports it.

Chapter Summary

In this chapter, we described setting performance standards based on rubrics to answer the question "How good is good enough?" We looked at several ways in which performance standards are set for district, state, and national assessments—"after the fact," "predefined," "relative," and "absolute" methods. We also explored grading as a means of setting performance standards in the classroom. Two sound procedures for converting rubric scores to grades were presented along with one questionable procedure to avoid.

BOX 5.4   Converting Rubric Scores to Grades

Don't: Do not add up all the points earned and divide by the number of points possible to get a percentage.

Do: Develop a logic rule for converting the descriptions associated with each score point to a grade that reflects a performance standard.

CHAPTER 6

Teaching Performance Criteria to Students

Guiding Question: How can we use rubrics to improve, as well as judge, student performance?

I t's all well and good to say that assessment and instruction should be integrated, or that students need to know and understand performance criteria. But such pronouncements are pretty useless unless we provide some actual examples of how it looks in the classroom when teachers and students are using rubrics and criteria to improve learning.

This chapter is devoted to the premise that performance criteria and rubrics can be powerful instructional tools for improving the very achievement that is also being assessed. Instruction and learning is the important link—the "so what" of all the rest—the reason why we're spending all this time on performance criteria and rubrics in the first place. The idea is simple—teach students the criteria for quality and how to apply them to their own work to make it better.

We begin with a discussion of what it takes to "know" criteria and then present seven practical strategies to assist students to "know" and understand criteria as a means of improving their achievement.

Remember the story in Chapter 1 about the conversation with the DMV in Washington State? That example illustrated the importance of knowing the criteria by which we are judged. And now for the rest of the story . . .

So, what does it take to *know* criteria for the driver's examination? Is it enough just to have the criteria handed to you when you climb into the driver's seat to be examined? "Oh, by the way, here are the criteria by which your driving will be judged. Good luck." Of course not.

So, what does it take to *know* criteria? Take a minute to reflect on this question. Then look at the comments in Box 6.1 to see how your comments overlap with those of other teachers.

> **BOX 6.1   To "know" criteria requires:**
>
> ■ Being exposed to the criteria from the beginning of instruction. (Having student-friendly versions that are given students during the first week of school.)
>
> ■ Having terms defined. (Include lots of details to describe the indicators of quality performance.)
>
> ■ Having examples of strong and weak performance illustrated by teacher modeling, student work samples, videos, etc. (Anonymous, of course.)
>
> ■ Practicing with feedback using the vocabulary of the criteria to suggest to students how to improve a piece of work.
>
> ■ Having opportunities for self- and peer assessment using the vocabulary of the criteria. (Letting students practice giving and receiving criterion-based feedback.)
>
> ■ Practicing articulating the vocabulary for quality and applying it to many situations. ("Dear Mom and Dad—Here's what I know about how to write well.")
>
> ■ Having instruction consciously focused on subparts of the criteria. (For example, in writing, focusing teaching on idea development, organization, voice, word choice, sentence fluency, and conventions.)

How does the vignette in Box 6.2 illustrate these principles? In this example, we see the integration of several principles described in this book.

1. The performance target is clear and doesn't move, providing an instructional target for the teacher and a learning target for the students.

2. There is no "mystery" regarding the performance expectations and the criteria by which student work will be judged.

3. The student work samples equip students to more accurately self-assess and improve their work before it is turned into the teacher.

The teacher has observed that the "target bulletin board" has sharpened her teaching and led to improvements in the quality of her students' work. We think that this example illustrates the productive blending of assessment and instruction. After all, isn't the primary purpose of assessment to promote learning, not simply measure it?

All of these ideas for teaching criteria to students have been consolidated by the staff at Northwest Regional Educational Laboratory (NWREL) into seven strategies outlined in Figure 6.2. Since NWREL has worked mostly with writing assessment, these seven strategies, and the accompanying examples in the rest of the chapter, relate to writing. However, the basic strategies presented below are applicable to virtually any performance area. As you look at the strategies applied in writing, think about how they might apply to your

BOX 6.2   Vignette: Making the Target Clear: Linking Assessment and Instruction

A middle-school language arts teacher has a large bulletin board in her classroom to which she has affixed a full-size archery target (obtained from the physical education department). At the start of each major unit of study, she directs the students to the bulletin board and discusses the "target" for the unit—the major goals and the rationale for learning this body of knowledge.

As part of the unit introduction, she discusses the culminating performance task that students will complete during the unit. On the bulletin board, she has mounted a large version of the rubric (or rubrics) that will be used in judging student performance on the final task, and she reviews the criteria with the students.

Now for the really cool part—she places examples of student work products collected from previous years (with student names removed) on the bulletin board. The work samples, which vary in quality, are connected to the different levels of the rubric and target. These provide tangible illustrations of the criteria and performance levels.

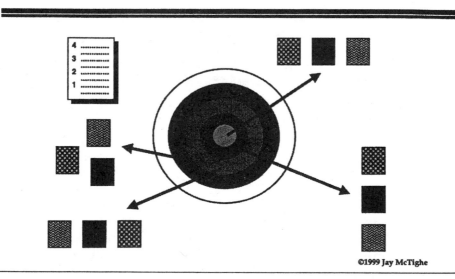

example:
a model bulletin board

©1999 Jay McTighe

Figure 6.1. Example of a Model Bulletin Board
© 1999, Jay McTighe.

Throughout the unit, the teacher uses the student examples along with the criteria in the rubric to support her teaching. In fact, she uses the good and poor samples to help students understand the nature of quality.

1. Teach students the LANGUAGE they need to speak and think like writers.

2. Read, score, and discuss ANONYMOUS sample papers.

3. PRACTICE AND REHEARSE focused revision strategies by

   ◆ Working with a partner or small group.

   ◆ Working on an ANONYMOUS sample.

   ◆ Revising for one trait at a time.

4. Read, Read, READ
   Printed material of ALL kinds to illustrate
   strengths and weaknesses in writing

5. WRITE!!
   Yes, WRITE—this means **you**! Then, ask students to help you
   revise your own writing for one of the traits.

6. Let students practice what they know.

7. TEACH FOCUS LESSONS
   Link YOUR curriculum to the traits as many ways and as
   many times as you can!

Figure 6.2. 7 Strategies for Teaching Writing Traits to Students
SOURCE: © 2000, NWREL. Portland, OR; 503-275-9500. Used with permission.

teaching areas—Critical thinking? Problem solving? Oral presentations? Collaborative group work? Other?[1]

This chapter just touches the surface of these ideas. Additional resources providing more detailed explanation and examples are given in the Resource section that follows this chapter.

Strategy 1: Teach Students the Language They Need to Think and Speak Like Writers

Have you ever used or observed peer review groups? Have you ever given them up because they seem to be unproductive—student comments to each other are very superficial? For example: "I like this, it's about dogs." "Your handwriting is neat."

1. Ask students what they like in the books they read. What draws them to one book or another? Begin making a list of features on the board.

2. Read a couple of age-appropriate (short) books to the students. After each book ask them if this gives them any additional ideas on what makes writing good. Add these to the list on the board.

3. Read a couple of anonymous student papers from last year, or use *The Redwoods* and *Fox* in Figure 6.4. Ask students to work in groups to decide which is the better paper. Have them list the reasons why they like one paper better than the other. Add their comments to the list on the board.

4. Tell the students that they have a pretty good list of features and ask them if they'd like to see what teachers value in writing.

5. Show students lists of teacher comments (Figure 6.5) and how similar they are to the students'. Students are always amazed at the similarity of the lists. For many of them, this is the first hint that they can also "be in on" the secret of the characteristics of quality.

6. Tell students that this year you're going to teach them how to look for and use the same criteria for quality writing that teachers use when they grade writing.

Figure 6.3. What to Do on Day 1

SOURCE: © 2000, NWREL. Portland, OR; 503-275-9500. Used with permission.

Maybe students don't make more insightful comments because they didn't know what to say to each other. They didn't know what features to look for in work to comment on. And, even if they did notice something, maybe they lacked the vocabulary for talking about it. Teaching students the criteria for quality teaches students what to notice and provides them a vocabulary for talking about it.

Teaching criteria is like teaching a foreign language—you need immersion. Surround students with the language of the criteria. Like the example of the teacher with the target on the bulletin board, provide students with pictures, examples, verbal descriptions, and models.

Figure 6.3 provides a step-by-step procedure for how you can start the immersion process for quality writing criteria.

Give students a copy of one of the "Student Friendly" versions of the rubric. (An elementary version of the Six-Traits + 1 Model is provided in the Resource section.) And you're on your way.

The Redwoods

Last year, we went on a vacation and we had a wonderful time. The weather was sunny and warm and there was lots to do, so we were never bored.

My parents visited friends and took pictures for their friends back home. My brother and I swam and also hiked in the woods. When we got tired of that, we just ate and had a wonderful time.

It was exciting and fun to be together as a family and to do things together. I love my family and this is a time that I will remember for a long time. I hope we will go back again next year for more fun and an even better time than we had this year.

Fox

I don't get along with people to good, and sometimes I am alone for a long time. When I am alone, I like to walk to forests and places where only me and the animals are. My best friend is God, but when I don't believe he's around sometime's, my dog stands in. We do every thing together. Hunt, fish, walk, eat and sleep together. My dog's name is Fox, 'cause he looks like an Arctic Fox. Fox and I used to live in this house with a pond behind. That pond was our property. The only thing allowed on it (that we allowed) was ducks & fish. If another person or dog would even look like going near that place, Fox and I would run them off in a frenzy. There was a lot of rocks around, so I would build forts and traps for any body even daring to come near. The pond had a bridge that was shaded by willows, so on a hot day me and Fox would sit on that bridge & soak our feet, well, I would soak my feet, Fox just kinda jumped in.

At night, the pond was alive with frogs, so I would invite this kid over, (he was a guy like me) and catch frogs. After we had a couple each, we would pick the best looking one out of our group and race them. The winner gets the other guys frog.

In the winter, the pond would freeze over, and I got my iceskates out. The pond was now an ice skating rink. Fox would chase me as I went round & round the pond.

After about a year, I was riding my bike patroling the area around the pond. With Fox at my side, I raced downhill toward the pond. I tried to stop, but my back tire went into a skid. I went face first into murky, shadowy waters. When I went down, a minute later I felt something pull on my shirt, I grabbed it, not knowing what to think, when I hit the surface, I saw that it was Fox, pulling on my shirt as if he was trying to save me. He was to little to save me if I was really drowning, but it was the thought that counts, I owe him one.

(continued)

Figure 6.4. The Redwoods and Fox

Another year passed. One day my mom got home from the store, and she bought me a rubber raft. It was just a cheap one, but it was mine. I blew it up with a tire pump. It was just the right size for me & Fox. Out of respect for Fox, I named it the USS Fox and christened it right in the pond.

On sunny days, I would take the raft out & lay in the sun with Fox on my legs. One day, when I was asleep in the raft, the wind blew pretty hard and blew my raft right into a bunch of sticks and rocks, the USS Fox was given a sad salute, and then was no more.

Another year passed, and this would be our last year by the pond. I admired and respected that pond more than I ever did that year. But, at long last, all good things must come to an end, we moved to another town. Fox & I still visit the pond, but it'll never be like them 3 years when she was mine.

Figure 6.4   Continued

Strategy 2: Read and Score Anonymous Student Papers

Strategy 2 helps students practice what to look for in writing that makes it work. Focus on the traits one by one. Students feel overwhelmed when they have to attend to all the features of good writing at once—remember the golf example in Chapter 2.

Teachers usually begin with the trait of Ideas. After all, a paper without good ideas is not worth reorganizing, improving word choice, and so on. Then, continue on to Organization, or perhaps Voice. Some teachers, however, prefer to begin with an easier trait to conceptualize, like Word Choice, in order to familiarize students with the use of criteria before moving on to more complex features of writing.

Spend as much time on each trait as students need—there's always next year. Our experience shows that by Grade 6, students can internalize all six traits in a single school year (a couple of hours a week). High school students can do it in a single term (again, a couple of hours a week). Adults take about 18 hours.

In any case, Figure 6.6 shows the steps in reading and scoring anonymous papers in order to internalize each component of quality.

Strategy 3: Practice-Focused Revision

While Strategies 1 and 2 assist students in practicing what to notice about quality, Strategy 3 helps them understand

IDEAS . . .

➡ Makes sense.

➡ Gets and holds my attention.

➡ Has a main idea, thesis, center, sense of purpose.

➡ Writer draws on experience.

➡ Says something new, or says it in a fresh way.

➡ Full of details that add.

➡ Important information.

➡ Interesting.

ORGANIZATION . . .

➡ The opening makes me want to keep reading.

➡ Has a logical order or pattern.

➡ I can follow the story or main points.

➡ Ends well. Ties up loose ends. Doesn't stop abruptly.

➡ Doesn't repeat what I just read: "Now you know the three reasons we should fight pollution."

➡ Pacing is good.

VOICE . . .

➡ Sounds like a person wrote it.

➡ Sounds like this *particular* writer.

➡ Writing has style, flavor.

➡ Reaches out to me, the reader. Brings me "inside."

➡ Makes me respond. Makes me *feel.*

WORD CHOICE . . .

➡ Makes me say, "Yes, that's just the right word or phrase!"

➡ Long after reading, some words still tug at my memory.

➡ Words are used correctly.

➡ The writer chooses wisely but isn't afraid to stretch.

➡ This writer knows the language of the topic—but doesn't try to impress me with phony, bloated phrases.

➡ Simple language is used when it gets the job done.

SENTENCE FLUENCY . . .

➡ It's smooth going—easy on the ear.

➡ I could *easily* read this aloud.

➡ Sentences begin differently. OR . . .

➡ Repetition is stylistic, not annoying.

➡ Some sentences are long. Some aren't.

➡ Sentences aren't choppy.

➡ Sentences don't meander.

CONVENTIONS . . .

➡ The writing is clean and polished. It looks proofread.

➡ *Most* things are done correctly.

➡ Careful, controlled use of conventions makes meaning clear and reading easy.

➡ No BIG erers sHoutt at me frm the pg: Hey!" Fergt IDEAS and VIOCE! Think ? abowt, the mystakes!, A lot!!"

➡ Spelling, punctuation, grammar, capital letters, and paragraph indenting: This writer has thoughtfully attended to ALL conventional details.

Figure 6.5. What Teachers Look for in Writing
SOURCE: © 2000, NWREL. Portland, OR; 503-275-9500. Used with permission.

This procedure should sound pretty familiar to anyone who has scored performance assessments. The procedure for teaching students to score papers is exactly the same as that for teaching adult raters.

1. Make overheads of sample *anonymous* student papers. Use papers from another teacher, from last year's students, or contact NWREL.

2. Read each paper out loud. Writing plays differently to the ear than it looks to the eye.

3. Focus on a single trait. Ask students to read their rubric for the focus trait and determine a score. Poll the students on their scores. Remember, there is no such thing as a "right" score, only a justifiable score. Scores should be justified by statements in the rubric. Have students articulate the statements that justify their score. If students disagree, ask them to try to convince each other that they are right, using the language of the rubric.

4. Students, as well as adult raters, might want to focus on "following directions." This might be important in some contexts, but not here. Keep emphasizing that it is the quality of the writing that counts, not whether students followed directions.

5. Read and score 6 to 8 papers for a single trait. Keep going until students are getting pretty good agreement rates on their scores. This might occur over several days, depending on the grade level.

Figure 6.6. Strategy 2: Teaching Traits by Scoring Anonymous Sample Papers
SOURCE: © 2000, NWREL. Portland, OR; 503-275-9500. Used with permission.

what to fix and how to fix it once a weakness has been noticed. Again, focus only on a single trait at a time (at least at first) because it is difficult for students to attend to everything that needs to be revised at once. Figure 6.7 describes how to have students practice focused revision.

Strategy 4: Read, Read, READ!

Use picture books and other literature to illustrate the traits—both strong and weak examples. Teachers have always read to students. But here's the difference when using Strategy 4: Purposely tie the selections back to one of the traits. Be explicit, using the language of the rubric. For example,

- For Voice, you might choose two versions of the same fairy tale written by different authors and ask students to notice differences between the voices. What is the voice? Frivolous, sad, excited, mocking, . . . ?

Again, use anonymous papers. Choose papers that really need revision on a particular trait. Don't do this just once. Do this 8 or 9 times on a single trait before moving on to the next trait.

1. Ask the students to score the paper on the target trait using their rubric (as in Strategy 2). Once again, ask students to justify their scores.

2. Have students brainstorm the things the author could do to make the paper better on this trait. For example, for the trait of ideas, students will often say: narrow the focus; add more details on the important points; take out details on unimportant points; choose one really interesting thing and expand on it; show, don't tell; and so on.

3. Have students work in groups to rewrite the piece using their own advice.

4. Ask groups to read their new versions aloud and justify why the new paper should get a higher score.

5. It often happens that revision on one trait—say, ideas—will also improve the other traits as well. Point this out to students.

6. After students have practiced revision on anonymous papers, ask them to revise one of their own pieces of writing for the trait being emphasized.

Figure 6.7. Strategy 3: Practice Focused Revision
SOURCE: © 2000, NWREL. Portland, OR; 503-275-9500. Used with permission.

- For Organization, you might ask students to compile a notebook of effective beginnings and endings, with descriptions of what makes them effective.

- For Sentence Fluency, choose books that are flowing, choppy, or have other types of sentence fluency. Ask students to describe the various styles and why the author chose the style he or she used. What purpose did it serve? What feel did it give to the writing?

Strategy 5: Model the Writing Process Yourself

Ask students to be a peer review group for your own writing. Don't pick a piece of writing that you've already revised. Pick a rough draft. Students often don't get to see that we, as teachers, don't have

1. Tell the students a story about something exciting that happened to you. Did your brakes go out on a hill? Were you charged by a lion in Africa? Make it interesting to capture their attention. Then tell them that you're going to share a written version of the story with them tomorrow.

2. Spend about 15 minutes writing up your story. Don't spend longer than that or it will be too good. You want to show the students a piece of writing that needs revision.

3. Read your story to the students, have them tell you what trait you need to work on first, and ask them to give you suggestions on how to make your paper better on that trait. They usually have a lot to say—they love to critique the teacher.

4. Use their suggestions to write a revision. Don't make it too good. Ask students to score the revision on the trait of interest and ask for additional suggestions. You need to model the fact that writing sometimes needs more than a single revision.

Keep going until students are satisfied with your paper. Point out that revising a paper for a single trait frequently also improves the other traits as well.

Figure 6.8. Model Revision
SOURCE: © 2000, NWREL. Portland, OR; 503-275-9500. Used with permission.

perfect writing springing from our pens on the first try. We also have to revise. Model it. In fact, the worse the first draft, the better. That will give students more to notice. Figure 6.8 describes a procedure that seems to work pretty well.

Strategy 6: Give Students Many Opportunities to Show What They Know

Here are a few examples to get you started. What else could you ask students to do to show what they know?

- Ask students to write letters to their favorite authors explaining, using the language of the traits, why they like the authors' work.

- Have students write to younger students about what it takes to write well. They need to explain the traits in language the younger students can understand.

- Have students work in teams to develop a poster that explains one of the traits. Use pictures, metaphors, and definitions.

- Ask students to analyze one of their own pieces of writing, using the language of the traits.
- Ask students to describe to their parents what they've learned this year in writing, using the language of the traits.

Strategy 7: Teach Lessons Focused on the Traits

This one is easy. You probably already have a file cabinet full of lessons and activities that teach one or more of the traits. The difference now is that you can organize them purposefully by trait, so that for every lesson you and the students will know the feature of good-quality writing that is being practiced. These can include the following:

1. Short "touch-up" activities to reinforce the traits. For example, teach different ways to organize expository writing and tie it to the trait of organization. Teach spelling, grammar, and other conventions.

2. Teach longer, more extensive lessons centered on the traits. For example, students usually need assistance in improving on their ideas. You can do a series of activities that help student improve their ideas. For example,

   a. Share six ways writers add drama to their writing—action, dialogue, description of setting, physical description of character, internal thinking of one of the characters, and internal physical sensations of one of the characters. Find examples. Practice.

   b. Describe and show the difference between showing and telling in writing. Find examples from literature. Have students practice turning telling into showing and showing into telling. Have discussions on when and how each could/should be used.

Chapter Summary

In this chapter we explored seven strategies for inviting students into the secrets of quality by teaching them criteria (see Box 6.3). The extended example was in writing, but we invited you to think about other subject areas.

> **BOX 6.3   Seven Strategies for Teaching Criteria to Students—In a Nutshell**
>
> The seven strategies can be summarized in one phrase: Surround students with the language they need to think and speak like writers (or problem solvers, critical thinkers, collaborators, etc.).

Final Thoughts

You've seen it all—from soup to nuts about rubrics: what they are, the types, when to use various types, what constitutes good ones, how to develop them, how to grade using them, and how to make quality real to students by teaching *them* the criteria for quality. What you have to remember is that even though all this information has come from many years of research and practice, it's still a continuous process of learning about rubrics—a process in which *we all* are still engaged! **These aren't the final answers—they're temporary answers until we all learn more.**

But it's also true that the ideas in this book—making learning targets clear to students and improving student achievement by inviting them into the assessment process—are not a flash in the pan. This is the future of assessment in education. Rubrics are a powerful means to this end.

Note

1. For example, we used some of these same strategies in Chapter 4 to teach you, the reader, criteria for good-quality rubrics. Which strategies did we use?

Rubrics Galore

Introduction

These rubrics are some of our favorites. They represent various grade levels and subject areas. They're here for two reasons. First, they're referenced throughout the book to illustrate points made. Second, in our experience, educators are desperate to get their hands on good ones. So, we've allocated a good portion of the book to these samples. None of these rubrics is perfect; all should be considered works in progress. Every one has some feature of interest. We've added a little annotation to each rubric below to make the interesting features clear.

Mathematics		
Rubric	*Description*	*Resource Page Numbers*
California Mathematics	Holistic, 6-point scale, Grades 4–12	pp. 98–100
Central Kitsap Student Friendly Guide to Mathematics Problem Solving	Analytical trait, 3 traits, student-friendly language, 5-point scale, Grades 4–9	pp. 101–107
Illinois Mathematics	Analytical trait, 3 traits, 5-point scale, Grades 4–9	pp. 108–109
NWREL Mathematics	Analytical trait, 5 traits, 4-point scale with "3" defined ahead of time as "proficient," Grades 3–12	pp. 110–111

Reading		
Rubric	*Description*	*Resource Page Numbers*
Juneau Reading Developmental Continuum	Analytical trait, 3 traits, continuous progress developmental continuum, 11 levels, Grades 1–5	pp. 112–117
NWREL Informational Reading	Analytical trait, 6 traits, 5-point scale, Grades 3-12	pp. 118–120
Oregon Reading	Analytical trait, 4 traits, 6-point scales, Grades 4–12, performance standard set after the rubric was developed ("4" or "5," depending on the trait and grade level)	pp. 121–125

Writing		
Rubric	*Description*	*Resource Page Numbers*
Maryland Scoring Rubric for Language in Use	Holistic, 3-point scale	p. 126
NAEP Primary Trait Rubrics	Primary trait, 6-point scale	pp. 127–129
NWREL Six-Trait + 1 Rubric for Assessing Writing—Adult and Student-Friendly versions	Analytical trait, 6 traits, 5-point scale, Grades 3–12, student-friendly language	pp. 130–143
Wauwatosa Developmental Continuum in Writing	Holistic, continuous progress developmental continuum, 11 levels, Grades K–5	pp. 144–156

Miscellaneous		
Rubric	*Description*	*Resource Page Numbers*
ATI Group Discussion Rubric	Analytical trait, 4 traits, 5-point scale, Grades 5–12	pp. 157–160
General Conceptual Understanding Rubric	Holistic, 3-point scale, Grades 5–12	pp. 161–162
Massachusetts Oral Presentation	Analytical trait, 4 traits, 4-point scale, Grades 5–12	pp. 163–168
Assessing "Intellectual Quality" of Student Work	Analytical trait, 3 traits, 4-point scale, Grades 6–12	pp. 169–176
Rubrics for Information-Processing Standards	Interprets and synthesizes information, uses a variety of information-gathering techniques, accurately assesses the value of information, recognizes how/where projects will benefit from new information	pp. 177–178

CALIFORNIA MATHEMATICS RUBRIC

As described in the *California Mathematics Framework* (1992), mathematically powerful students are those who can draw on mathematical ideas, tools, and techniques to think and communicate. In responding to an open-ended question and accomplishing its task, a student demonstrates mathematical power. As the student engages in and responds to the task, he or she draws from his or her thinking capacity, understanding of mathematical ideas, ability to use tools and techniques, communication skills, and ability to shape a coherent and focused response.

The general rubric below is used to evaluate responses to open-ended questions in mathematics. The rubric articulates the extent to which student work accomplishes the purpose of the task and demonstrates mathematical understanding, reasoning, thinking, communicating, and use of tools and techniques. Level 6 represents the highest quality of work, and Level 1 the lower quality of performance. This rubric can be applied to any open-ended task. Therefore, before applying this rubric to mathematics assessment, the scorer must explore all possible ways in which it relates to a particular problem. In other words, the scorer looks for the mathematical ideas, thinking, communication, tools, and techniques that a student can use to solve a particular problem.

Level 6: Solid work that may go beyond the requirements of the task(s), showing, for example,

- Complete understanding of the task's mathematical concepts and processes

- Clear identification of all of the important elements of the task(s)

- Where appropriate, clear evidence of doing purposeful mathematics, including investigating, experimenting, modeling, designing, interpreting, analyzing, or solving

- Excellent prose and mathematical supporting arguments that may include examples or counterexamples

- Creativity and thoughtfulness in communicating the results and the interpretations of those results, to an identified audience, using dynamic and diverse means

- Multiple solutions based on different assumptions about or interpretations of the task(s)

- Unusual insights into the nature of and the resolution of problems encountered in the task(s)

SOURCE: Reprinted from *A Sampler of Mathematics Assessment–Addendum.* © 1994, California Department of Education. Used with permission.

- A high level of mathematical thinking that includes, where appropriate, making comparisons, conjectures, interpretations, predictions, or generalizations
- Exceptional skill in choosing appropriate mathematical tools and techniques in the resolution of problems in task(s)

Level 5: Fully achieves the requirements of the task(s), showing, for example,

- Good understanding of the task's mathematical concepts and processes
- Identification of most, if not all, of the important elements of the task(s)
- Evidence of doing purposeful mathematics, including where appropriate, investigating, experimenting, modeling, designing, interpreting, analyzing, or solving
- Clear, successful communications with an identified audience
- One solution and interpretation of those results
- Evidence of mathematical thinking that includes, where appropriate, making comparisons, conjectures, interpretations, predictions, or generalizations
- Use of variety of tools and techniques appropriate to the form of the task(s) and the requirements of the task

Level 4: Substantially completes the requirements of the task(s), showing, for example,

- An understanding of most of the task's mathematical concepts and processes
- Identification of the important elements of the task(s), but some less important ideas are missing
- Some aspects of investigations, experiments, model building, designs, interpretations, analysis, solutions required by the task(s) may be missing, but most are included
- Adequate communication with an identified audience, but with limited clarity and variety
- Occasional evidence of mathematical thinking involving comparisons, conjectures, interpretation, predictions, or generalizations
- A limited variety of tools and techniques used to resolve the situation presented in the task(s)

SOURCE: Reprinted from *A Sampler of Mathematics Assessment–Addendum.* © 1994, California Department of Education. Used with permission.

Level 3: Limited completion of the requirements of the task(s), showing for example,

- An understanding of some of the task's mathematical concepts and processes, but with evidence of gaps in those understandings
- Identification of some of the important elements of the task(s), but assumptions about some of the elements may be flawed
- Communication of some ideas, but generally makes inadequate attempts to communicate, often failing to address the identified audience, and difficulty in expressing mathematical ideas
- Inadequate mathematical thinking that includes ineffective analysis procedures, limited solution strategies, unclear mathematical arguments, and inappropriate interpretation of results
- A selection of some inappropriate tools and techniques used to resolve the situation presented in the task(s)

Level 2: Requirements of the task(s) not completed, showing, for example,

- Only fragmented understanding of the task's mathematical concepts and processes, accompanied by disorganized, incomplete results
- Identification of only a few, usually superficial, elements of the task(s)
- Attempts to address the intended audience that may be incoherent, muddled, or incomplete
- Attempts to explain or justify results that are convoluted, illogical, circular, or unrelated to the results shown

Level 1: Does not achieve any requirements of the task(s), showing, for example,

- An irrelevant, nonsensical, or illegible response that has no valid relationship to the task(s)

- No understanding of the task's mathematical concepts and processes
- Unsuccessful attempt, if any, to communicate with the intended audience
- Usually communication is not attempted
- No attempt to explain or justify results. If attempt is made, it is often unrelated to the task, illegible, or incoherent

---

SOURCE: Reprinted from *A Sampler of Mathematics Assessment–Addendum.* © 1994, California Department of Education. Used with permission.

The Student Friendly Guide to Mathematics Problem Solving

Central Kitsap School District
P.O. Box 8
Silverdale, WA 98383
Curriculum Department
(360) 692-3101

SOURCE: Curriculum Department, Central Kitsap School District. Used with permission.

Mathematical Knowledge
Concepts and Procedures

The student understands mathematical concepts and performs related operations, chooses the appropriate math operations, and performs computations correctly.

➤ Understands the mathematical ideas and operations selected
➤ Performs appropriate computations
➤ Chooses the right operations and does them correctly

SOURCE: Curriculum Department, Central Kitsap School District. Used with permission.

Mathematical Concepts and Procedures

> 5   I completely understand the appropriate mathematical operation and use it correctly.

➤ I understand which math operations are needed.

➤ I have used all of the important information.

➤ I did all of my calculations correctly.

> 3   I think I understand most of the mathematical operations and how to use them.

➤ I know which operations to use for some of the problem but not for all of it.

➤ I have an idea about where to start.

➤ I know what operations I need to use, but I'm not sure where the numbers go.

➤ I picked out some of the important information, but I might have missed some.

➤ I did the simple calculations right, but I had trouble with the tougher ones.

> 1   I wasn't sure which mathematical operation(s) to use or how to use the ones I picked.

➤ I don't where to start.

➤ I'm not sure which information to use.

➤ I don't know which operations would help me solve the problem.

➤ I don't think my calculations are correct.

SOURCE: Curriculum Department, Central Kitsap School District. Used with permission.

Problem Solving

> **The student selects and carries out a strategy to find a solution, and checks results for reasonableness.**

> ➤ Translates the problem into mathematical terms
> ➤ Chooses or creates a strategy
> ➤ Uses a strategy to solve the problem
> ➤ Checks solution to make sure it make sense in the problem

---

Some Strategies for Problem Solving

Draw a picture or diagram.

Look for patterns.

Use trial and error.

Make a table.

Work with special cases, then generalize.

Try simpler numbers.

Work backwards from the solution.

SOURCE: Curriculum Department, Central Kitsap School District. Used with permission.

Problem Solving

> **5   I came up with and used a strategy that really fits and makes it easy to solve this problem.**

➤ I know what to do to set up and solve this problem.

➤ I knew what math operations to use.

➤ I followed through with my strategy from beginning to end.

➤ The way I worked the problem makes sense and is easy to follow.

➤ I may have shown more than one way to solve the problem.

➤ I checked to make sure my solution make sense in the original problem.

> **3   I came up with and used a strategy, but it doesn't seem to fit the problem as well as it should.**

➤ I think I know what the problem is about, but I might have a hard time explaining it.

➤ I arrived at a solution even though I had problems with my strategy at some point.

➤ My strategy seemed to work at the beginning but did not work well for the whole problem.

➤ I checked my solution and it seems to fit the problem.

> **1   I didn't have a plan that worked.**

➤ I tried several things but didn't get anywhere.

➤ I didn't know which strategy to use.

➤ I didn't know how to begin.

➤ I didn't check to see if my solution makes sense.

➤ I'm not sure what the problem asks me to do.

➤ I'm not sure I have enough information to solve the problem.

SOURCE: Curriculum Department, Central Kitsap School District. Used with permission.

Communication

> The student explains the process, reasoning, and strategy used in solving the problem.

➤ Explains the strategy and processes used.

➤ Explains why what was done was done.

➤ Explains why answer works.

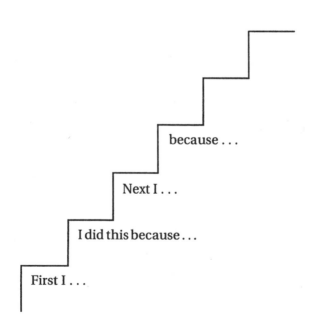

because . . .

Next I . . .

I did this because . . .

First I . . .

SOURCE: Curriculum Department, Central Kitsap School District. Used with permission.

Communication

> | 5 | I clearly explained the process I used and my solution to the problem using numbers, words, pictures, or diagrams. |

- ➤ My explanation makes sense.
- ➤ I used mathematical terms correctly.
- ➤ My work shows what I did and what I was thinking while I worked the problem.
- ➤ I've explained why my answer makes sense.
- ➤ I used pictures, symbols, and/or diagrams when they made my explanation clearer.
- ➤ My explanation was clear and organized.
- ➤ My explanation includes just the right amount of detail, not too much or too little.

> | 3 | I explained in words part of the process I used, or I only explained my answer. |

- ➤ I explained some of my steps in solving the problem.
- ➤ Someone might have to add some information for my explanation to be easy to follow.
- ➤ Some of the math vocabulary I used makes sense and help in my explanation.
- ➤ I explained my answer but not my thinking.
- ➤ My explanation started out well but bogged down in the middle
- ➤ When I used pictures, symbols, and/or diagrams, they were incomplete or only helped my explanation a litle bit.
- ➤ I'm not sure how much detail I need in order to help someone understand what I did.

> | 1 | I did not explain my thinking or my answer, or I am confused about how my explanation relates to the problem. |

- ➤ I don't know what to write.
- ➤ I can't figure out how to get my ideas in order.
- ➤ I'm not sure I used math terms correctly.
- ➤ My explanation is mostly copying the original problem.
- ➤ The pictures, symbols, and/or diagrams I used would not help someone understand what I did.

SOURCE: Curriculum Department, Central Kitsap School District. Used with permission.

MATHEMATICS SCORING RUBRIC: A GUIDE TO EXTENDED-RESPONSE ITEMS

The following rubric is used for the extended-response items for all grade levels.

Score Level	*MATHEMATICAL KNOWLEDGE:* *Knowledge of mathematical principles and concepts which result in a correct solution to a problem.*	*STRATEGIC KNOWLEDGE:* *Identification of important elements of the problem and the use of models, diagrams, symbols, and/or algorithms to systematically represent and integrate concepts.*	*EXPLANATION:* *Written explanation and rationales that translate into words the steps of the solution process and provide justification for each step. Though important, length of the response, grammar, and syntax are not the critical elements of this dimension.*
4	• Shows complete understanding of the problem's mathematical concepts and principles • Uses appropriate mathematical terminology and notions including labeling answer, if appropriate; that is, whether or not the unit is called for in the stem of the item • Executes algorithms completely and correctly	• Identifies all the important elements of the problem and shows complete understanding of the relationships among elements • Reflects an appropriate and systematic strategy for solving the problem • Solution process is nearly complete	• Gives a complete written explanation of the solution process employed; explanation addresses both *what* was done and *why* it was done • If a diagram is appropriate, there is a complete explanation of all the elements in the diagram
3	• Shows nearly complete understanding of the problem's mathematical concepts and principles • Uses nearly correct mathematical terminology and notations • Executes algorithms completely; computations are generally correct but may contain minor errors	• Identifies most of the important elements of the problem and shows general understanding of the relationship among them • Reflects an appropriate strategy for solving the problem • Solution process is nearly complete	• Gives a nearly complete written explanation of the solution process employed, or explains *what* was done and begins to address *why* it was done • May include a diagram with most of the elements explained

	Mathematical Knowledge	Strategic Knowledge	Explanation
2	• Shows some understanding of the problem's mathematical concepts and principles • May contain major computational errors	• Identifies some important elements of the problem but shows only limited understanding of the relationship among them • Appears to reflect an appropriate strategy but the application of strategy is unclear, or a related strategy is supplied logically and consistently • Gives some evidence of a solution process	• Gives some written explanation of the solution process employed; either explains *what* was done or addresses *why* it was done; explanation is vague or difficult to interpret • May include a diagram with some of the elements explained
1	• Shows limited to no understanding of the problem's mathematical concepts and principles • May misuse or fail to use mathematical terms • May contain major computational errors	• Fails to identify important elements or places too much emphasis on unimportant elements • May reflect an inappropriate or inconsistent strategy for solving the problem • Gives minimal evidence of a solution process; process may be difficult to identify	• Gives minimal written explanation of solution process; may fail to explain *what* was done and *why* it was done • Explanation does not match presented solution process • May include minimal discussion of elements in diagram; explanation of significant element is unclear
	• No answer attempted	• No apparent strategy	• No written explanation of the solution process is provided

SOURCE: From *Illinois Standards Achievement Test: Sample Mathematics Materials 2000* (p. 59). © 2000, Illinois Department of Public Instruction. Used with permission.

MATHEMATICS SCORING RUBRIC

	Emerging	Developing	Proficient	Exemplary
Conceptual Understanding **Key Question:** Does the student's interpretation of the problem using mathematical representations and procedures accurately reflect the important mathematics in the problem?	1. Your mathematical representations of the problem were incorrect. 2. You used the wrong information in trying to solve the problem. 3. The mathematical procedures you used would not lead to a correct solution. 4. You used mathematical terminology incorrectly.	1. Your choice of forms to represent the problem was inefficient or inaccurate. 2. Your response was not completely related to the problem. 3. The mathematical procedures you used would lead to a partially correct solution. 4. You used mathematical terminology imprecisely.	1. Your choices of mathematical representations of the problem were appropriate. 2. You used all relevant information from the problem in your solution. 3. The mathematical procedures you chose would lead to a correct solution. 4. You used mathematical terminology correctly.	1. Your choice of mathematical representations helped clarify the problem's meaning. 2. You uncovered hidden or implied information not readily apparent. 3. You chose mathematical procedures that would lead to an elegant solution. 4. You used mathematical terminology precisely.
Strategies and Reasoning **Key Question:** Is there evidence that the student proceeded from a plan, applied appropriate strategies, and followed a logical and verifiable process toward a solution?	1. Your strategies were not appropriate for the problem. 2. You didn't seem to know where to begin. 3. Your reasoning did not support your work. 4. There was no apparent relationship between your representations and the task. 5. There was no apparent logic to your solution. 6. Your approach to the problem would not lead to a correct solution.	1. You used an oversimplified approach to the problem. 2. You offered little or no explanation of your strategies. 3. Some of your representations accurately depicted aspects of the problem. 4. You sometimes made leaps in your logic that were hard to follow. 5. Your process led to a partially complete solution.	1. You chose appropriate, efficient strategies for solving the problem. 2. You justified each step of your work. 3. Your representation(s) fit the task. 4. The logic of your solution was apparent. 5. Your process would lead to a complete, correct solution of the problem.	1. You chose innovative and insightful strategies for solving the problem. 2. You proved that your solution was correct and that your approach was valid. 3. You provided examples and/or counterexamples to support your solution. 4. You used a sophisticated approach to solve the problem.

Category / Key Question				
Computation and Execution **Key Question:** Given the approach taken by the student, is the solution performed in an accurate and complete manner?	1. Errors in computation were serious enough to flaw your solution. 2. Your mathematical representations were inaccurate. 3. You labeled incorrectly. 4. Your solution was incorrect. 5. You gave no evidence of how you arrived at your answer.	1. You made minor computational errors. 2. Your representations were essentially correct but not accurately or completely labeled. 3. Your inefficient choice of procedure impeded your success. 4. The evidence for your solution was inconsistent or unclear.	1. Your computations were essentially accurate. 2. All visual representations were complete and accurate. 3. Your solution was essentially correct. 4. Your work clearly supported your solution.	1. All aspects of your solution were completely accurate. 2. You used multiple representations for verifying your solution. 3. You showed multiple ways to compute your answer.
Communication **Key Question:** Was I able to easily understand the student's thinking, or did I have to make inferences and guesses about what they were trying to do?	1. I couldn't follow your thinking. 2. Your explanation seemed to ramble. 3. You gave no explanation for your work. 4. You did not seem to have a sense of what your audience needed to know. 5. Your mathematical representations did not help clarify your thinking.	1. Your solution was hard to follow in places. 2. I had to make inferences about what you meant in places. 3. You weren't able to sustain your good beginning. 4. Your explanation was redundant in places. 5. Your mathematical representations were somewhat helpful in clarifying your thinking.	1. I understood what you did and why you did it. 2. Your solution was well organized and easy to follow. 3. Your solution flowed logically from one step to the next. 4. You used an effective format for communicating. 5. Your mathematical representations helped clarify your solution.	1. Your explanation was clear and concise. 2. You communicated concepts with precision. 3. Your mathematical representations expanded on your solution. 4. You gave an in-depth explanation of your reasoning.
Insights **Key Question:** Does the student grasp the deeper structure of the problem and see how the process used to solve this problem connects it to other problems or "real world" applications?	1. You were unable to recognize patterns and relationships. 2. You found a solution and then stopped. 3. You found no connections to other disciplines or mathematical concepts.	1. You recognized some patterns and relationships. 2. You found multiple solutions, but not all were correct. 3. Your solution hinted at a connection to an application or another area of mathematics.	1. You recognized important patterns and relationships in the problem. 2. You found multiple solutions using different interpretations of the problem. 3. You connected your solution process to other problems, areas of mathematics, or applications.	1. You created a general rule or formula for solving related problems. 2. You related the underlying structure of the problem to other similar problems. 3. You noted possible sources of error or ambiguity in the problem. 4. Your connection to a real-life application was accurate and realistic.

SOURCE: © 2000, Northwest Regional Educational Laboratory, Portland, OR; 503-275-9500. Permission granted for use in the classroom.

READING DEVELOPMENTAL CONTINUUM
LEARNING TO READ, LEARNING TO LISTEN

	LEVEL A PRE-EMERGENT	LEVEL B EMERGENT	LEVEL C BEGINNING
Comprehension	• Uses pictorial cues when sharing a book or "reading" (e.g., points to a picture in The Three Little Pigs and says, "The three little pigs left home." • Talks about favorite stories. • Demonstrates understanding of television programs, oral stories or picture books by connecting them to own knowledge and experiences.	• May tell a story from pictures. • Predicts meaning of environmental symbols or messages (e.g., recurrent "Stop" signs, McDonald's symbol, etc). • Tells/draws personal stories in sequence. • Listens to and retells stories in sequence.	• Recognizes when the reading isn't making sense. • Recounts sequence of events. • Listens to stories and responds. *Mark continuum based on secure habituated, independent behavior of student
Skills/Strategies	• Recognizes own name in a variety of print. • Displays reading-like behavior: –holds the book the right way up –turns the pages appropriately –looks at words and pictures –uses pictures to construct ideas • Understands that print is read from top to bottom of page and left page before right page. • Responds to and uses simple terminology such as: book, right way up, front, back, upside down.	• Recognizes most letter sounds. • Recognizes parts of own name in print (e.g., Sam says, "That's in my name" pointing to 'Stop' sign). • Knows several words by sight (mom, I, stop, dad, friends' names). • Relies primarily on memory for reading. • May invent text with book language. • Focuses on pictures for meaning rather than print. • Knows that both pictures and text exist. • Understands that print is read from left to right on a page.	• Uses initial and/or final letter and sounds to predict a word. • Locates/reads known words (sight words). • Begins to use context, grammatical, and/or phonics cues. • Matches words spoken to words in print (1-1 match). • Stops at an unknown word. • Looks at print and pictures. • Understands the difference between a sentence, word, letter. • Understands that print carries meaning. • Knows concepts of beginning, middle, and end. • Begins to read in phrases as opposed to word by word.

112

Attitudes/Behaviors		
• Displays curiosity about print by experimenting with scribble writing and drawing and asking, "What does that say?" • Looks at books. • Chooses and enjoys hearing a variety of favorite books. • Eagerly responds to book-reading events (plays, flannel board, puppets).	• Asks questions or comments about print in the environment. • Actively participates in the oral/shared reading of familiar stories (e.g., joins in on familiar refrains, patterns, or phrases in books or poems). • Wants to read text and points to text in general. • May pretend to read.	• Is willing to read. • Focuses on print, supported by pictures. • Vocalizes when reading. • Uses appropriate listening behaviors.

KINDERGARTEN RANGE: A to C

FIRST GRADE RANGE : B–F

SOURCE: © 2000, Juneau Borough School District, Juneau, AK. Used with permission.

LEARNING TO READ, LEARNING TO LISTEN

	LEVEL D EARLY DEVELOPING	LEVEL E DEVELOPING	LEVEL F
Comprehension	• Predicts what will happen next. • Recalls main ideas and details. • Orally connects own experiences to reading.	• Retells story in sequence. • Summarizes story. • Backs up literal statements with proof from story. • Forms an opinion about a story.	• Orally responds to questions about character, setting, problem, and solution. • Understands the use of exaggeration. • Distinguishes fact from fiction. • Demonstrates knowledge of the function of chapters.
Skills/Strategies	• Uses word parts to read unknown words (e.g., endings—s, ed, ing; blends—sp, bl, st; digraphs—ch, sh, th; and simple word families— . . . at, . . . ad, . . . op). • Increases sight word vocabulary. • Increases and refines use of context, grammatical, and/or phonics cues. • Begins to use a variety of ways of cross checking. • Begins to self-correct errors. • Pauses at appropriate places when reading orally. • Uses a period, question mark, and exclamation mark when reading.	• Begins to solve unknown words by using word families (. . . ate, . . . eat, . . . een, etc). • Uses beginning, middle and final letter sounds to read unknown word. • Increases sight word vocabulary. • Cross checking is automatic. • When rereading, confidently reads a story with appropriate expression. • Uses quotation marks and commas when reading.	• Solves unknown words by using syllables or meaningful word parts (e.g., root words—tie, do, read; prefixes—un, re, pre; and suffixes—ful, ly, est). • Increases sight word vocabulary. • Self-corrects automatically. • Reads orally with expression or with appropriate pauses.

114

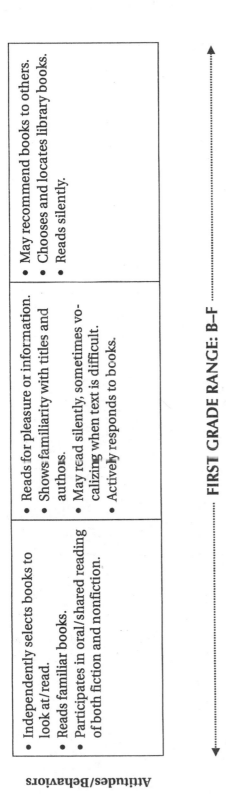

Attitudes/Behaviors

• Independently selects books to look at/read. • Reads familiar books. • Participates in oral/shared reading of both fiction and nonfiction.	• Reads for pleasure or information. • Shows familiarity with titles and authors. • May read silently, sometimes vocalizing when text is difficult. • Actively responds to books.	• May recommend books to others. • Chooses and locates library books. • Reads silently.

········· **FIRST GRADE RANGE: B–F** ·········

———— **SECOND GRADE RANGE: D to H** ————

SOURCE: © 2000, Juneau Borough School District, Juneau, AK. Used with permission.

LEARNING TO READ, LEARNING TO LISTEN / READING TO LEARN, LISTENING TO LEARN

	LEVEL G	LEVEL H BENCHMARK 3	LEVEL I
Comprehension	• Orally responds to literature questions and is beginning to respond in writing. • Identifies and interprets characters' interactions. • Recognizes and retains specialized vocabulary (e.g., unusual names, unfamiliar terms/concepts). • Understands idiomatic expressions (. . . fur looked like mashed prunes). • Retains story line through episodes or longer chapter books. *Mark continuum based on secure habituated, independent behavior of student	• Summarizes major events. • Identifies character, setting, and plot. • Evaluates characters, authors, and books. • Uses information to draw conclusions. • Recalls word meaning by giving an example. • Notices author's choices of words. • Compares ideas read to prior knowledge. • Listens and responds orally to others' opinions and questions about a text. • Knows how to question self before, during, and after reading.	• Connects ideas to make inferences, draw conclusions, and predict what will happen next. • Recalls word meanings by giving a definition. • Recognizes effective use of word choice by an author for a specific purpose. • Listens and responds to fiction and nonfiction in writing, discussions, storytelling/performance, and so forth. • Interprets fiction read by retelling and discussing plot, characters, setting, and events. • Interprets nonfiction, citing main ideas and supporting details. • Paraphrases/retells passages. • Supports opinions about text with evidence from text and own life.

Skills/Strategies	• Uses word identification strategies appropriately and automatically when encountering an unknown word.
	• Retains high frequency words as part of sight word vocabulary.
		• Integrates reading strategies fluently and effectively.
		• Reads contractions and abbreviations. Identifies and uses:
		  –title page
		  –table of contents
		  –index
		  –author, illustrator
		• Adjusts reading rate to meet the demands of the text.
			• Rereads, scans, and skims text for specific information.
			• Analyzes parts of words and sentence context to problem-solve new words.
			• Uses references for specific research purposes.
			• Uses text organizations such as chapters, paragraphs, and conclusions.
			• Identifies and uses:
			  –glossary
			  –copyright.

Attitudes/ Behaviors	• Chooses to read a variety of materials for a variety of purposes. • Uses active listening skills during oral reading of fiction and nonfiction.	• Knows own reading preferences. • Selects texts at his/her reading level.	• Reflects and evaluates self as a reader. • Self-motivated to read for pleasure.

SECOND GRADE RANGE: D to H

THIRD GRADE RANGE: G to I

FOURTH GRADE RANGE: H to K

FIFTH GRADE RANGE: I to K

SOURCE: © 2000, Juneau Borough School District, Juneau, AK. Used with permission.

READING TO LEARN, LISTENING TO LEARN

LEVEL J	LEVEL K BENCHMARK 5
• Makes inferences based on ideas in text ustification for the inferences. • Begins to use content vocabulary in speaking and writing. • Recognizes that authors use specific words to convey a feeling, tone, and emotional state. • Connects ideas from reading to universal themes such as friendship, tolerance, and community.	• Comprehends texts that may be removed from personal experience. • Begins to use content vocabulary in reference to real life situations. • Interprets author's use of specific words/phrases that convey feeling, tone, and emotional states. • Identifies figurative language such as simile, metaphor, onomato-poeia, and alliteration. • Recognizes devices in a text that indicate stereotyped characters and suggests ways in which stereotypical characters might be changed. • Compares universal themes between texts read. • Infers, predicts, and generalizes, citing evidence from the text. • Confirms, extends, or amends own knowledge through reading.
• Selects and uses a variety of reference materials for specific research purposes. • Uses a variety of text structures (letter, narrative, report, recount) and text organizations (bold print, key word, caption).	• Selects appropriate material and adjusts reading strategies for different texts and purposes (skimming to search for a fact, scanning for a key word, headings). • Reads and uses content-specific vocabulary (e.g., in science, math, technology).
• Generates personal questions and discussion about self as a reader. • May discover a particular genre and may seek out other titles of this type.	• Analyzes self as a reader. • Sees books as useful sources of information.

———— FOURTH GRADE RANGE: H to K ·······················

———— FIFTH GRADE RANGE: I to K ·······················

SOURCE: © 2000, Juneau Borough School District, Juneau, AK. Used with permission.

THE TRAITS OF AN EFFECTIVE READER:
READING AN INFORMATIONAL TEXT SCORING GUIDE

Decoding Conventions

- Decode the writing *conventions* of grammar, punctuation, word recognition, and sentence structure
- Recognize the organizational *conventions* of the author, the organizational framework, and features of the text
- Identify the genre *conventions* (newspaper, magazine, textbooks, brochures, instructions) and the types of modes appropriate to each informational genre (cause and effect, comparison, sequential, etc)

5 The advanced response uses conventions information to form a confident "thinking frame" of a text.
- Directly answers the question using text structure language in specific and precise ways
- Selects well-chosen and well-supported examples to illustrate understanding of conventions
- Responds "beyond" the question by enlarging the initial thinking frame

3 The developing response uses conventions information to form an initial "thinking frame" of the text.
- Uses some basic text structure language to indicate general understandings
- Selects "safe" and obvious examples to illustrate understanding of the conventions
- The response is fairly safe and stays definitely within the confines of the question

Establishing Comprehension

- Identify and explain the vocabulary key to the main thesis of the text
- Identify the main idea, major and minor examples, facts, expert authority, and turning moments
- Distinguish between significant and supporting details that elaborate the main idea
- Summarize and paraphrase with purpose to move toward making inferences and interpretations

5 The advanced response demonstrates a purposeful, expansive, and knowledgeable comprehension of the text.
- Directly answers the question using comprehension terms to indicate precise understandings
- Selects well-chosen examples to illustrate in-depth comprehension; examples are well-developed, using clear, specific language, and terms
- Responds "beyond" the question by increasing comprehension of the text into inferential and interpretive levels

3 The developing response demonstrates an adequate comprehension of the text. Purposeful comprehension is still evolving.
- Uses some comprehension terms to indicate general understandings
- Selects "safe" and obvious examples to illustrate literal comprehension
- Does not venture information beyond the initial question

Realizing Context

- Identify the time period and its accompanying social realities in the text
- Recognize the perspective–point of view–of the text and its relationship to social factors
- Identify the vocabulary reflective of the context
- Recognize the writing mode, tone, and voice of the author or source selected with respect to the context
- Recognize the subject matter's context and its applications to many aspects of the text

5 The advanced response realizes context and sees inferential meanings and intended purposes, both implicit and explicit.
- Directly and specifically answers the question to demonstrate understanding of inferential meaning
- Selects well-chosen examples to illustrate understandings of contextual issues
- Goes beyond the question's limits to illustrate understandings of contextual relationships

3 The developing response realizes the context of the text to some degree and recognizes obvious types of inference. The idea of contextual relationships between many factors and issues is still in development.
- Uses some context terminology to show a basic level of understanding
- Selects "safe" and obvious examples that stay close to the surface of the text
- Stays within the safe confines of the question

(continued)

Decoding Conventions

1 The emerging response is beginning to decode conventions and the challenge of decoding gets in the way of a "thinking frame" for the text.

- Does not adequately answer the question but may use some text structure language
- Focuses on more general information rather than providing examples from the text
- Response can be characterized as sketchy and incomplete

Developing Interpretations

- Identify problems, gaps, ambiguities, conflicts, and/or disparate points of view in the text
- Analyze the text to pose explanations that bridge gaps, clarify ambiguities, and resolve textual problems
- Using the context to connect analytical explanations to a bigger picture

5 The advanced response interprets to analyze and think critically about informational texts.

- Directly answers the question by employing problem-solving techniques—using specific evidence, clues, and "on target" information
- Examples, quotes, and events are cited from the text and connected strongly to the analysis
- Responds beyond the question to engage the bigger picture by creating framework of historical significance, cultural importance, or universal theme

Establishing Comprehension

1 The emerging response is searching to establish a basic comprehension of the text.

- Does not provide examples for evidence but sometimes restates the question
- Little evidence that a basic comprehension of the text has been achieved
- The response can be characterized as sketchy and incomplete

Integrating for Synthesis

- Put information in order to explain the text's process or chronology
- Compare and contrast examples, facts, or events in order to make defensible judgments or interpretations
- Recognize and describe cause and effect relations
- Integrate personal experience, background knowledge, and/or content knowledge with the text to create a "synthesis" of text plus knowledge

5 The advanced response integrates textual material and other types of knowledge to create a synthesis of ideas.

- Directly, specifically, and concretely performs the synthesis application directed by the question by using synthesis language
- Uses well-chosen examples that have a strong parallel development if the question demands it
- Responds beyond the question, integrating several layers of knowledge into a harmonious whole

Realizing Context

1 The emerging response guesses at context but has difficulty accessing inferential knowledge.

- Does not use examples from the text to illustrate inferential understandings
- Not enough evidence to demonstrate an understanding of contextual layers of the text

Critiquing for Evaluation

- Experiment with ideas in the text
- Express opinions about the text
- Raise questions about the text
- Make good judgments about the text by using a synthesis of material derived from interpretation
- Challenge the ideas of the author or source by noting bias, distortion, and/or lack of coherence
- Contrast the accuracy of textual information with other sources and form solid, defensible critiques

5 The advanced response evaluates to assert a strong voice in the text.

- Directly and thoughtfully answers the question, using evaluation terminology effectively and precisely to indicate the reader's critique of the text
- Examples are well-developed, placed in context, and connected well to other ideas
- Responds beyond the parameters of the question to critically engage the text and its ideas in a solid, defensible judgment

(continued)

SOURCE: © 2000, Northwest Regional Educational Laboratory, Portland, OR; 503-275-9500. Used with permission.

THE TRAITS OF AN EFFECTIVE READER (continued)

Developing Interpretations	Integrating for Synthesis	Critiquing for Evaluation
3 The developing response interprets to expand the text but is still developing connections to a larger worldview.	**3 The developing response integrates textual material with other types of knowledge to create a surface-level synthesis.**	**3 The developing response hesitates to evaluate thoroughly; it still plays it somewhat "safe."**
• Uses some language that indicates an initial layer of interpretation understanding	• Uses some synthesis language to reflect a basic understanding of the skills of integrating for synthesis	• Generally answers the evaluation question but hesitant to critically engage with the text
• A safe response citing very obvious examples; connections between the examples and the analysis not always evident	• Uses general and "safe" examples	• Selects safe and obvious examples that are connected to other ideas in fairly limited ways
• Does not yet move beyond the question—engaging the "bigger picture" is still a developing skill	• The layers and types of knowledge in the response not always well integrated	• Does not yet move beyond the question to venture into the larger world of critical discourse
1 The emerging response sees interpretation as "talking about a book." Reading and interpreting are still separate processes. Little evidence exists that the student understands the concept of interpretation.	**1 The emerging response employs some skills of synthesizing, but a fully developed integration is still emerging.**	**1 The emerging response is just beginning to explore a critical stance to the text.**
• Does not adequately address the question	• Does not perform the synthesis application directed by the question	• Uses evaluation terminology sporadically or not at all
• Does not cite examples, quotes, or evidence from the text to use as a basis of interpretation	• Does not accurately use synthesis language	• Examples are incomplete or sketchily described and not connected to other ideas or issues
• Sometimes restates the question words	• Does not integrate sources, texts, and understandings to a measurable degree	• The response is incomplete or restates the question words

SOURCE: © 2000, Northwest Regional Educational Laboratory, Portland, OR; 503-275-9500. Used with permission.

READ – INFORMATIVE AND LITERARY TEXTS / OFFICIAL SCORING GUIDE, GRADES 4-12
Comprehension

6 The response demonstrates a thorough understanding of the parts of the selection and the selection as a whole.

The response:
- Indicates a thorough and accurate understanding of main ideas and all significant supporting details, including clarification of the complexities
- Draws subtle as well as obvious inferences and forms insightful conclusions about their meaning
- Presents interpretation, generalizations, or predictions based on specific and compelling evidence
- Uses relevant and specific information from textual resource (e.g., table of contents, graphs, charts, diagrams, glossary) to clarify meaning and form conclusions.

5 The response demonstrates a strong understanding of the parts of the selection and the selection as a whole.

The response:
- Indicates a thorough and accurate understanding of main ideas and all significant supporting details
- Draws key inferences and forms supported conclusions about their meaning
- Presents interpretations, generalizations, or predictions based on specific, conclusive evidence
- Uses information from textual resources (e.g., table of contents, chapter headings, graphs, charts, diagrams) to clarify meaning and form conclusions.

4 The response demonstrates a competent understanding of the parts of the selection and the selection as a whole.

The response:
- Indicates an understanding of the main ideas and relevant and specific supporting details
- Draws obvious inferences and forms reasoned conclusions about their meaning
- Presents interpretations, generalizations, or predictions based on adequate evidence
- Uses information from textual resources (i.e., table of contents, chapter headings, illustrations, graphs, charts) to clarify meaning and form conclusions.

3 The response demonstrates an inconsistent understanding of the parts of the selection and the selection as a whole.

The response:
- Correctly identifies some main ideas; focuses on isolated details or misunderstands or omits some significant supporting details
- Draws basic inferences but may not provide supportable conclusions based on them
- Attempts to present interpretations, generalizations, or predictions but fails to provide adequate support
- Uses obvious information from textual resources (i.e., table of contents, chapter headings, illustrations, graphs, charts).

2 The response demonstrates a limited understanding of the parts of the selection and the selection as a whole.

The response:
- Shows a fragmented, inaccurate, or incomplete understanding of the selection; presents random, incomplete, or irrelevant evidence
- Does not draw inferences or suggests inferences not supported by the text
- Fails to provide supported interpretations, generalizations, or predictions or provides ones that are unsupported by the text; may contain passages copied verbatim without analysis or commentary
- Does not refer to textual resource (e.g., table of contents, graphs, charts, diagrams, glossary) or reveals that the reader is distracted or confused by them.

1 The response demonstrates virtually no understanding of the parts of the selection and the selection as a whole.

The response:
- Shows an inability to construct a literal meaning of the selection; may focus only on the reader's own frustration or indicate that the reader gave up.

(continued)

SOURCE: © 1997, Oregon Department of Education. Used with permission.

6 **The response demonstrates a thorough and complex understanding of the selection and the selection and it relationship to other texts (read, heard, or viewed), experiences, issues, or events in the community or world at large.**
The response:
- Relates the selection to substantive and relevant personal experience, extending understanding and deepening understanding beyond text-bound concerns.
- Relates the selection to other texts in complex and subtle ways through insightful generalization or conclusions.
- Makes insightful and supported connections between theme(s) or message(s) of a selection(s) and its relationship to issues or events in the community or world at large.

5 **The response demonstrates a strong understanding of the selection and its relationship to other texts (read, heard, or viewed), experiences, issues, or events in the community or world at large.**
The response:
- Relates the selection to relevant personal experiences, extending understanding beyond text-bound concerns.
- Relates the selection to other texts in complex and subtle ways through supported generalizations or conclusions.
- Makes in-depth connections between theme(s) or message(s) of a selection(s) and issues or events in the community or world at large.

4 **The response demonstrates a competent understanding of the selection and its relationship to other texts (read, heard, or viewed), experiences, issues, or events in the community or world at large.**
The response:
- Relates the selection to relevant personal experiences, extending understanding beyond text-bound concerns.
- Relates the selection to other texts by drawing conclusions or forming generalizations although they may be primarily literal.
- Makes reasoned connections between theme(s) or message(s) of a selection(s) and issues or events in the community or world at large.

3 **The response demonstrates an limited or inconsistent understanding of the selection and its relationship to other texts (read, heard, or viewed), experiences, issues, or events in the community or world at large.**
The response:
- Relates the selection only superficially or indirectly to personal experiences.
- Relates the selection to other texts by drawing conclusions or forming generalizations which may be simplistic or incomplete.
- Makes overly broad, general, or inaccurate connections between the selection(s) and issues or events in the community or world at large.

2 **The response demonstrates a limited, superficial, or flawed understanding of the selection and its relationship to other texts (read, heard, or viewed), relevant personal experiences, or related topics or events.**
The response:
- Relates the selection only superficially or indirectly to personal experiences.
- Makes weak or invalid connections between the selection and other texts.
- Makes weak or superficial connections between the selection(s) and issues or events in the community or world at large.

1 **The response demonstrates a lack of understanding of the selection and its relationship to other texts (read, heard, or viewed), relevant personal experiences, or related topics or events.**
The response:
- Shows an inability to draw connections and see relationship between the selection and other texts, experiences, issues, and events.

Reading Critically: Text Analysis

6 The response demonstrates a thorough and convincing analysis and evaluation of an author's ideas and craft. *The response:* • Identifies the author's purpose and presents a thorough and insightful analysis and evaluation of how the author's stylistic decisions (e.g., structure, point of view, word choice) affect the message and purpose. • When based on a literary text, identifies and skillfully analyzes how literary elements (i.e., character, plot, setting, theme) and/or devices (e.g., simile, metaphor, symbol) contribute tot he unity and effectiveness of the text. • Uses specific and relevant evidence from the text to make reasoned judgments about the author's craft and the selection's explicit or implied message(s).	**5 The response demonstrates a strong understanding of the parts of the selection and the selection as a whole.** *The response:* • Identifies the author's purpose and presents an analysis and evaluation of how some of the author's stylistic decisions (e.g., structure, point of view, word choice) impact the message and purpose. • When based on a literary text, analyzes how selected literary elements (i.e., character, plot, setting, theme) and/or devices (e.g., simile, metaphor, symbol) contribute to the unity and effectiveness of the text • Uses specific and relevant evidence from the text to make reasoned judgments about the author's craft and the selection's explicit or implied message.
4 The response demonstrates a competent analysis and evaluation of an author's ideas and craft. *The response:* • Identifies the author's purpose and analyzes how the author's stylistic decisions (e.g., structure, point of view, word choice) contribute to the purpose. • When based on a literary text, provides a basic analysis of how literary elements (e.g., character, plot, setting, theme) and/or literary devices (e.g., simile, metaphor, symbol) contribute to the unity and effectiveness of the selection. • Uses relevant evidence from the text to make and support reasoned judgments about the author's craft and the selection's explicit message; may respond to implied messages.	**3 The response demonstrates an incomplete analysis of an author's ideas and craft but provides simplistic or unsupported evaluations of the author's ideas and craft.** *The response:* • Show's limited identification and analysis of the author's purpose and begins to analyze how stylistic decisions (e.g., structure, point of view, word choice) contribute to the messages. • When based on a literary text, gives unsupported or simplistic explanations of how literary elements or devices contribute to overall effectiveness of the selection. • Uses limited evidence from the text to form opinions about the author's craft and explicit message; may respond to implied messages.
2 The response demonstrates a limited, confused, or unfounded analysis of the author's ideas and craft. *The response:* • Indicates a lack of awareness of the author's purpose or stylistic decisions; there may even be an apparent lack of awareness of the author's voice (i.e., the reader may seem to have difficulty distinguishing author from narrator or character in the selection). • When based on a literary text, does not use literary terms (e.g., character, plot, symbol, metaphor) to describe the effectiveness of the selection. • Makes a judgment about the author's craft or message(s) but provides r o textual support.	**1 The response demonstrates no evidence of critical reading skills; the reader does not engage in a thoughtful analysis of the text.** *The response:* • Reflects an unquestioned acceptance or rejection of the author's craft or text's message(s) without comment or explanation.

(continued)

SOURCE: © 1997, Oregon Department of Education. Used with permission.

READ OFFICIAL SCORING GUIDE (continued)

Reading Critically: Context Analysis

6 The response demonstrates a thorough and convincing analysis and evaluation of the ways in which an author's message(s) or theme(s) have influenced or have been influenced by history, society, culture, and life experiences.
The response:
- Applies a comprehensive understanding of an author's life experiences to evaluate how they have shaped and influenced the author's work.
- When appropriate, recognizes and evaluates the complex and subtle ways in which a selection(s) has had an impact on past and/or present social and cultural conditions and issues.
- Uses extensive knowledge and understanding about social, economic, political, or cultural issues and events to analyze and evaluate the validity of the selection's explicit or implied theme(s) or message(s); if appropriate, proposes more than one interpretation of the text.

5 The response demonstrates a strong analysis and evaluation of the ways in which an author's message(s) or theme(s) have influenced or have been influenced by history, society, culture, and life experiences.
The response:
- Applies an understanding of an author's life experiences to evaluate how they have shaped and influenced the author's work.
- When appropriate, recognizes and analyzes the ways in which a selection(s) has had an impact on past and/or present social and cultural conditions and issues.
- Uses knowledge and understanding about social, economic, political, or cultural issues and events to analyze the validity of the selection's explicit or implied theme(s) or message(s); if appropriate, proposes more than one interpretation of the text.

4 The response demonstrates a competent analysis and evaluation of the ways in which an author's message(s) or theme(s) have influenced or have been influenced by history, society, culture, and life experiences.
The response:
- Applies an understanding of an author's life experiences to examine and explain ways they have shaped and influenced the author's work.
- When appropriate, recognizes and analyzes the ways in which a selection has had an impact on past and/or present social and cultural conditions and issues; minor inaccuracies may occur.
- Uses knowledge and understanding about social, economic, political, or cultural issues and events to analyze the validity of the selection's explicit or implied theme(s) or message(s).

3 The response demonstrates an incomplete analysis of the ways in which an author's message(s) or theme(s) have influenced or have been influenced by history, society, culture, and life experiences.
The response:
- Applies a limited or incomplete understanding of an author's life experiences to examine and explain ways they have influenced the author's work.
- When appropriate, recognizes ways in which a selection(s) has had an impact on past and/or present social and cultural conditions and issues; the explanation may contain minor inaccuracies.
- Shows limited knowledge about social, economic, political, or cultural issues and events and relates knowledge to the selection's explicit theme(s) or message(s).

2 The response demonstrates a limited, confused, or unfounded analysis of the ways in which an author's message(s) or theme(s) have influenced or have been influenced by history, society, culture, and life experiences.
The response:
- Attempts in superficial or illogical ways to explain how an author's life experiences have influenced the author's work.
- When asked, attempts in superficial or illogical ways to explain how a selection has had an impact on social and cultural conditions and issues.
- Makes a judgment about the selection's message(s) or theme(s) but provides no contextual support.

1 The response demonstrates no evidence of critical reading skills; the reader does not engage in a thoughtful analysis of the text.
The response:
- Reflects an unquestioned acceptance or rejection of the text without comment or explanation.

SOURCE: © 1997, Oregon Department of Education. Used with permission.

SCORING RUBRIC FOR LANGUAGE IN USE

Score Point 3	Score Point 2
• Consistently uses word choices to express meaning with style and tone • Consistently uses word and sentence order to express meaning with style and tone • Consistently uses correct mechanics, spelling, capitalization, and punctuation (Errors that are present represent risk-taking but do not interfere with meaning.)	• Generally uses word choices to express meaning with style and tone • Sometimes uses word and sentence order to express meaning with style and tone • Generally uses correct mechanics, spelling, capitalization, and punctuation (Errors may or may not represent risk-taking but do not interfere with meaning.)
Score Point 1	
• Rarely uses word choices to express meaning with style and tone • Rarely uses word and sentence order to express meaning with style and tone • Only sometime uses correct mechanics, spelling, capitalization, and punctuation (Errors do not represent risk-taking and may interfere with meaning.)	

SOURCE: © 1994, Maryland Assessment Consortium. Used with permission.

PRIMARY TRAIT RUBRICS

Narrative Scoring Guide

In reading and evaluating the narrative papers, the scoring guide development team focused on several key features of narrative writing. First, they loosely defined a story as a series of related events or happenings. Hence, the first level of the narrative scoring guide is not termed a "story" but an *Event Description* because only one event is described.

1. **Event Description.** Paper is a list of sentences minimally related or a list of sentences that all describe a single event.

2. **Undeveloped Story.** Paper is a listing of related events. More than one event is described but with few details about setting, characters, or the event. (Usually, there is no more than one sentence telling about each event.)

3. **Basic Story.** Paper describes a series of events, giving details (in at least two or three sentences) about some aspect of the story (the events, the characters' goals, or problems to be solved). But the story lacks cohesion because of problems with syntax, sequencing, events missing, or an undeveloped ending.

4. **Extended Story.** Paper describes a sequence of episodes, including details about most story elements (i.e., setting, episodes, charters' goals, problems to be solved). But the stories are confusing or incomplete (i.e., at the end the characters' goals are ignored or problems inadequately resolved; the beginning does not match the rest of the story; the internal logic or plausibility of characters' actions is not maintained).

5. **Developed Story.** Paper describes a sequence of episodes in which almost all story elements are clearly developed (i.e., setting, episodes, characters' goals, or problems to be solved) with a simple resolution of these goals or problems at the end. May have one or two problems or include too much detail.

6. **Elaborated Story.** Paper describes a sequence of episodes in which almost all story elements are well developed (i.e., setting, episodes, characters' goals, or problems to be solved). The resolution of the goals or problems at the end are elaborated. The events are presented and elaborated in a cohesive way.

SOURCE: National Assessment of Educational Progress, 1992.

Informative Scoring Guide

In reading and evaluating the informative papers, the scoring guide development team focused on several key traits of informative writing. First, they loosely defined informative writing as the presentation of information and ideas for the purpose of informing an audience. Further, in the process of presenting information, the writer establishes relationships between pieces of information and/or ideas. The papers were then classified according to how well the writers had succeeded in establishing relationships and according to how well they presented the information to a particular audience for a specific purpose.

The differences between Levels 1 through 4 are the degree to which the writers established relationships between the pieces of information in their papers. The difference between Levels 5 and 6 is the degree to which the writers conveyed a sense of audience and purpose. This was often accomplished through the use of an overt type of organizational structure.

1 **Listing.** Paper lists pieces of information or ideas all on the same topic but does not relate them. A range of information/ideas is presented.

2 **Attempted Discussion.** Paper includes several pieces of information and some range of information. In part of the paper, an attempt is made to relate some of the information (in a sentence or two), but relationships are not clearly established because ideas are incomplete or undeveloped (the amount of explanation and details is limited).

3 **Undeveloped Discussion.** Paper includes a broad range of information and attempts to relate some of the pieces of information. The relationships are somewhat established but not completely. The ideas are confused, contradictory, out of sequence, illogical, or undeveloped.

4 **Discussion.** Paper includes a broad range of information and, in at least one section, clearly relates the information using rhetorical devices (such as temporal order, classification, comparison/contrast, cause and effect, problem/solution, goals/resolutions, predictions, speculations, suppositions, drawing conclusions, point of view, ranking exemplification).

5 **Partially Developed Discussion.** Paper includes a broad range of information and establishes more than one kind of relationship using rhetorical devices, such as those listed above. Information and relationships are well developed, with explanations and supporting details. Paragraphs are well formed but the paper lacks an overriding sense of purpose and cohesion.

6 **Developed Discussion.** Paper includes a broad range of information and establishes more than one kind of relationship using rhetorical devices, such as those listed above. Information and relationships are explained and supported. The paper has a coherent sense of purpose and audience and is free from grammatical problems. An overt organizational structure is used (such as the traditional essay format).

SOURCE: National Assessment of Educational Progress, 1992.

Persuasive Scoring Guide

In reading and evaluating the persuasive papers, the scoring guide development team focused on several key features of persuasive discourse: stating an opinion or position, supporting one's opinion with reasons and/or explanation, and attempting to diffuse or refute the opposing position. While developing an argument by clearly stating and supporting an opinion may be considered an effective way of persuading an audience, the team felt that papers which include the recognition and refutation of an opposing viewpoint are more complex forms of persuasion. They placed the 58 persuasive papers submitted by students along a continuum of persuasive complexity, ranging from opinion to argumentation to refutation.

1 **Opinion.** Paper is a statement of opinion, but no reasons are given to support the opinion, or the reasons given are inconsistent or unrelated to the opinion.

2 **Extended Opinion.** Paper states opinion and gives reasons to support the opinion, but the reasons are not explained or the explanations given are incoherent.

3 **Partially Developed Argument.** Paper states opinion and gives reasons to support the opinion, plus attempts to develop the opinion with further explanation. However, the explanations are given but not developed or elaborated. May contain a brief reference to the opposite point of view.

4 **Developed Argument.** Paper states opinion, gives reasons to support the opinion, plus explanations, with at least one explanation developed through the use of rhetorical devices (such as sequence of events, cause and effect, comparison/contrast, classification, problem/solution, point of view, drawing conclusions). May contain a brief summary of the opposite point of view.

5 **Partially Developed Refutation.** Paper states opinion, gives reasons to support opinion, explanations, plus attempts to discuss and/or refute the opposite point of view. Contains an adequate summary of the opposite point of view.

6 **Developed Refutation.** Paper states opinion, gives reasons to support opinion, explanations, plus a discussion and/or refutation of opposing point of view. Refutation is clear and explicit—summarizes opposite point of view and discusses why it is limited or incorrect.

SOURCE: National Assessment of Educational Progress, 1992.

6 + 1 TRAITS OF ANALYTICAL WRITING
ASSESSMENT SCORING GUIDE (RUBRIC)

WOW!

Exceeds expectations

○ **STRONG:**

shows control and skill in this trait; many strengths present

↓**COMPETENT:**

on balance, the strengths outweigh the weaknesses; a small amount of revision is needed

→**DEVELOPING:**

strengths and need for revision are about equal; about halfway home

↑**EMERGING:**

need for revision outweighs strengths; isolated moments hint at what the writer has in mind

←**NOT YET:**

a bare beginning; writer not yet showing any control

- **IDEAS**
- **ORGANIZATION**
- **VOICE**
- **WORD CHOICE**
- **SENTENCE FLUENCY**
- **CONVENTIONS**
- **PRESENTATION**

SOURCE: © 2000, Northwest Regional Educational Laboratory, Portland, OR; 503-275-9500. Permission granted for use in the classroom.
Note: The adult version of each trait is followed by the student-friendly (Grades 3-8) version.

IDEAS
(Development)

5 This paper is clear and focused. It holds the reader's attention. Relevant anecdotes and details enrich the central theme.

  A. The topic is *narrow* and *manageable.*

  B. *Relevant, telling, quality details* give the reader important information that goes *beyond the obvious* or predictable.

  C. Reasonably *accurate details* are present to support the main ideas.

  D. The writer seems to be writing from *knowledge* or *experience*; the ideas are *fresh* and *original.*

  E. The reader's questions are *anticipated and answered.*

  F. *Insight*—an understanding of life and a knack for picking out what is significant—is an indicator of high level performance, though not required.

3 The writer is beginning to define the topic, even though development is still basic or general.

  A. The *topic is fairly broad*; however, you can see where the writer is headed.

  B. *Support is attempted* but doesn't go far enough yet in fleshing out the key issues or story line.

  C. Ideas are *reasonably clear,* though may not be detailed, personalized, accurate, or expanded enough to show in-depth understanding or a strong sense of purpose.

  D. The writer seems to be drawing on knowledge or experience but has *difficulty going from general observations to specifics.*

  E. The reader is *left with questions.* More information is needed to "fill in the blanks."

  F. The writer *generally stays on the topic* but does not develop a clear theme. The writer has not yet focused the topic past the obvious.

1 As yet, the paper has no clear sense of purpose or central theme. To extract meaning from the text, the reader must make inferences based on sketchy or missing details. The writing reflects more than one of these problems:

  A. The writer is *still in search of a topic,* brainstorming, or has not yet decided what the main idea of the piece will be.

  B. Information is *limited* or *unclear* or the *length is not adequate* for development.

  C. The idea is a *simple restatement* of the topic or an *answer* to the question with little or no attention to detail.

  D. The writer has *not begun to define the topic* in a meaningful, personal way.

  E. *Everything seems as important as everything else;* the reader has a hard time sifting out what is important.

  F. The text may be *repetitious* or may read like a collection of *disconnected, random thoughts* with no discernable point.

IDEAS
—My Message—

It all makes sense.

My reader will learn a lot.

It's really clear.

Ready to share!

This is just what
I wanted to say.

Good, juicy details!

5

Halfway home! 4

You might have some questions.

It TELLS, but it doesn't SHOW.

My reader will get the general idea.

I need to add some details.

I'm working on it!

3

Just beginning 2

I'm afraid my reader won't follow this.

It's hard to get started.

I'm not sure what my topic is. . . OR, . . . maybe my topic is too BIG.

The picture is not very clear.

I need more time to think.

1

ORGANIZATION

5 The organization enhances and showcases the central idea or theme. The order, structure, or presentation of information is compelling and moves the reader through the text.

A. An *inviting introduction* draws the reader in; *a satisfying conclusion* leaves the reader with a sense of closure and resolution.

B. *Thoughtful transitions* clearly show how ideas connect.

C. Details seem to fit where they're placed; *sequencing is logical* and effective.

D. *Pacing is well-controlled*; the writer knows when to slow down and elaborate and when to pick up the pace and move on.

E. The *title*, if desired, is *original* and captures the central theme of the piece.

F. Organization *flows so smoothly* the reader hardly thinks about it; the choice of structure matches the *purpose* and *audience*.

3 The organizational structure is strong enough to move the reader through the text without too much confusion.

A. The paper has a *recognizable introduction and conclusion*. The introduction may not create a strong sense of anticipation; the conclusion may not tie up all loose ends.

B. *Transitions often work well*; at other times, connections between ideas are fuzzy.

C. *Sequencing* shows *some logic*, but not under control enough that it consistently supports the ideas. In fact, sometimes it is so predictable and rehearsed that the *structure takes attention away from the content*.

D. *Pacing is fairly well controlled,* though the writer sometimes lunges ahead too quickly or spends too much time on details that do not matter.

E. A *title (if desired) is present,* although it may be uninspired or an obvious restatement of the prompt or topic.

F. The *organization sometimes supports the main point or storyline*; at other times, the reader feels an urge to slip in a transition or move things around.

1 The writing lacks a clear sense of direction. Ideas, details, or events seem strung together in a loose or random fashion; there is no identifiable internal structure. The writing reflects more than one of these problems:

A. There is *no real lead* to set up what follows, no real conclusion to wrap things up.

B. Connections between ideas are *confusing* or not even present.

C. *Sequencing needs* lots and lots of *work*.

D. *Pacing feels awkward*; the writer slows to a crawl when the reader wants to get on with it, and vice versa.

E. *No title is present* (if requested), or if present, *does not match* well with the content.

F. Problems with organization make it *hard for the reader to get a grip* on the main point or story line.

SOURCE: © 2000, Northwest Regional Educational Laboratory, Portland, OR; 503-275-9500. Permission granted for use in the classroom.

ORGANIZATION
—From Beginning to End—

I know where I'm going

My opening will hook you!

The ending really works!

Ready to share!

Follow me!

I see just how all the parts fit together.

5

4 Halfway home!

Some pieces of my paper fot better than others.

My beginning is OK.

My paper is PRETTY easy to follow.

Maybe I need to move some things around.

The ending doesn't grab me yet.

3

How do I begin?

This is confusing.

2 Just beginning

What should I tell firsts? What comes next?

Help! Which pieces go together?

I don't know where I'm headed.

1

How do I end this?

VOICE

5 **The writer speaks directly to the reader in a way that is individual, compelling, and engaging. The writer crafts the writing with an awareness and respect for the audience and the purpose for writing.**

A. The tone of the writing *adds interest* to the message and *is appropriate for the purpose and audience.*

B. The reader feels a *strong interaction* with the writer, sensing the *person behind the words.*

C. The writer *takes a risk* by revealing who he or she is consistently throughout the piece.

D. *Expository or persuasive* writing reflects a *strong commitment* to the topic by showing *why* the *reader needs to know this* and why he or she should care.

E. *Narrative* writing is *honest, personal, engaging* and makes you *think about and react to* the author's ideas and point of view.

3 **The writer seems sincere but not fully engaged or involved. The result is pleasant or even personable, but not compelling.**

A. The writer seems aware of an audience but discards personal insights in favor of *obvious generalities.*

B. The writing communicates in an *earnest, pleasing, yet safe* manner.

C. Only *one or two moments here or there* intrigue, delight, or move the reader. These places may emerge strongly for a line or two but quickly fade away.

D. *Expository or persuasive* writing *lacks consistent engagement* with the topic to build credibility.

E. *Narrative* writing is *reasonably sincere* but doesn't reflect unique or individual perspective on the topic.

1 **The writer seems indifferent, uninvolved, or distanced from the topic and/or the audience. As a result, the paper reflects more than one of the following problems:**

A. The writer is *not concerned with the audience.* The writer's style is a *complete mismatch* for the intended reader, or the writing is so short that little is accomplished beyond introducing the topic.

B. The writer speaks in a kind of *monotone* that flattens all potential highs or lows of the message.

C. The writing is *humdrum and "risk free."*

D. The writing is *lifeless or mechanical*; depending on the topic, it may be overly technical or jargonistic.

E. The development of the topic is *so limited* that *no point of view is present*—zip, zero, zilch, nada.

VOICE
—Putting Myself in my Writing—

It's Me!!

This is what I think.

I'm speaking right to the reader.

It might make you laugh or cry.

Ready to share!

Hear me
ROAR!

I love this topic.

I want my reader to
feel what I feel.

5

Halfway home! 4

This topic is OK.

Sometimes I'm speaking
to the reader.

I'm starting to have fun.

I hear _a little_ of me
in the writing.

I'm hiding my feelings
and ideas a little.

3

I'm not speaking
to the
reader—_yet_.

Just beginning 2

I don't hear myself in this paper.

This topic is boring.

SNORE!

I wish I didn't have to do this.

1

WORD CHOICE

5 **Words convey the intended message in a precise, interesting, and natural way. The words are powerful and engaging.**

A. Words are *specific* and *accurate*; it is easy to understand just what the writer means.

B. The words and phrases *create pictures and linger in your mind.*

C. The language is *natural and never overdone*; both words and phrases are *individual* and *effective.*

D. *Striking words and phrases* often catch the reader's eye—and linger in the reader's mind. (You can recall a handful as you reflect on the paper.)

E. *Lively verbs* energize the writing. *Precise nouns and modifiers* add depth and specificity.

F. *Precision* is obvious. The writer has taken care to put just the right word or phrase in just the right spot.

3 **The language is functional, even if it lacks much energy. It is easy to figure out the writer's meaning on a general level.**

A. Words are *adequate and correct in a general sense*; they simply *lack much flair and originality.*

B. Familiar *words and phrases communicate* but rarely capture the reader's imagination. Still, the paper may have *one or two fine moments.*

C. *Attempts at colorful language* show a willingness to stretch and grow, but sometimes it goes too far (thesaurus overload!).

D. The writing is marked by *passive verbs, everyday nouns and adjectives, and lack of interesting adverbs.*

E. The words are only occasionally refined; it's more often *"the first thing that popped into my mind."*

F. The words and phrases are *functional*—with only a moment or two of sparkle.

1 **The writer struggles with a limited vocabulary, searching for words to convey meaning. The writing reflects more than one of these problems:**

A. Language is so *vague* (e.g., *It was a fun time; She was neat; It was nice; We did lots of stuff*) that only a *limited message* comes through.

B. *"Blah, blah, blah"* is all that the reader reads and hears.

C. *Words are used incorrectly,* making the message secondary to the misfires with the words.

D. *Limited vocabulary* and/or frequent *misuse of parts of speech* impair understanding.

E. *Jargon or clichés distract or mislead. Persistent redundancy* distracts the reader.

F. Problems with language *leave the reader wondering* what the writer is trying to say. The *words just don't work* in this piece.

SOURCE: © 2000, Northwest Regional Educational Laboratory, Portland, OR; 503-275-9500. Permission granted for use in the classroom.

WORDS

—Playing with Language—

My words paint a picture.

My words make the message CLEAR.

I love the way my
words sound and feel.

Ready to share!

I think this is the
BEST way to say it!

5

Halfway home! 4

I need more
IMAGINATION here!

These are some of the
first words I thought of.

Some of the words and phrases are
great, but some need some work.

There is probably a
BETTER way to say it.

3

2

Just beginning

Soem words
are really
vague.

These words are NOT my favorites.

The words I've used don't paint a picture in your mind.

Some of my words don't make sense
to me when I read them over.

1

SENTENCE FLUENCY

5 **The writing has an easy flow, rhythm, and cadence. Sentences are well built, with strong and varied structure that invites expressive oral reading.**

A. Sentences are constructed in a way that underscores and enhances the *meaning*.

B. Sentences *vary in length as well as structure*. Fragments, if used, add style. Dialogue, if present, sounds natural.

C. *Purposeful* and *varied sentence beginnings* add variety and energy.

D. The use of *creative and appropriate connectives* between sentences and thoughts shows how each relates to, and builds upon, the one before it.

E. The writing has *cadence*; the writer has thought about the sound of the words as well as the meaning. The first time you read it aloud is a breeze.

3 **The text hums along with a steady beat but tends to be more pleasant or businesslike than musical, more mechanical than fluid.**

A. Although sentences may not seem artfully crafted or musical, *they get the job done in a routine fashion*.

B. Sentences are *usually constructed correctly*; they *hang together*; they are *sound*.

C. *Sentence beginnings* are not ALL alike; *some variety is attempted*.

D. The reader sometimes has to *hunt for clues* (e.g., connecting words and phrases like *however, therefore, naturally, after a while, on the other hand, to be specific, for example, next, first of all, later, but as it turned out, although,* etc.) that show how sentences interrelate.

E. *Parts* of the text *invite expressive oral reading*; others may be stiff, awkward, choppy, or gangly.

1 **The reader has to practice quite a bit in order to give this paper a fair interpretive reading. The writing reflects more than one of the following problems:**

A. Sentences are *choppy, incomplete, rambling or awkward*; they need work. *Phrasing does not sound natural.* The patterns may create a sing-song rhythm or a chop-chop cadence that lulls the reader to sleep.

B. There is little to *no "sentence sense"* present. Even if this piece were flawlessly edited, the sentences would not hang together.

C. Many *sentences begin the same way*—and may follow the same patterns (e.g., *subject-verb-object*) in a monotonous pattern.

D. *Endless connectives* (*and, and so, but then, because, and then,* etc.) or a complete lack of connectives create a massive jumble of language.

E. The text *does not invite expressive oral reading*.

FLUENCY
—*Listening to the Sound*—

My paper is EASY to read out loud.

*Some sentences are LONG and STRETCHY—
some are SHORT and SNAPPY.*

Ready to share!

*My
sentences
begin in several
different ways.*

I love the sound of this paper—its got rhythm!

5

Halfway home! 4

*A lot of my sentences
begin the same way.*

3

*My sentences are all
about the same length.*

*I wish my paper sounded a
little smoother in places.*

*It's PRETTY easy to read out loud
if you take your time.*

Just beginning 2

Help! Some of these sentences don't make sense.

My paper is HARD to read out loud—even for me!

Sometimes, I can't tell where to begin a new sentence.

*I've got a problem—either (1) everything is strung
together is one endless sentence or (2) there are lots
of choppy little sentences, one after another.*

1

SOURCE: © Northwest Regional Educational Laboratory. Permission granted for use in the classroom.

CONVENTIONS

5 **The writer demonstrates a good grasp of standard writing conventions (e.g., spelling, punctuation, capitalization, grammar and usage, paragraphing) and uses conventions effectively to enhance readability. Errors tend to be so few that just minor touch-ups would get this piece ready to publish.**

A. *Spelling is generally correct,* even on more difficult words.

B. The *punctuation is accurate,* even creative, and guides the reader through the text.

C. A thorough understanding and consistent application of *capitalization* skills are present.

D. *Grammar and usage are correct* and contribute to clarity and style.

E. *Paragraphing tends to be sound* and reinforces the organizational structure.

F. The writer *may manipulate conventions* for stylistic effect—and it works! The piece is very close to being *ready to publish.*

GRADES 7 AND UP ONLY: The writing is sufficiently complex to allow the writer to show skill in using a wide range of conventions. For writers at younger ages, the writing shows control over those conventions that are grade/age appropriate.

---

3 **The writer shows reasonable control over a limited range of standard writing conventions. Conventions are sometimes handled well and enhance readability; at other times, errors are distracting and impair readability.**

A. *Spelling* is usually *correct or reasonably phonetic on common words,* but more difficult words are problematic.

B. *End punctuation is usually correct;* internal punctuation (*commas, apostrophes, semicolons, dashes, colons, parentheses*) is sometimes missing/wrong.

C. *Most words are capitalized correctly;* control over more sophisticated capitalization skills may be spotty.

D. *Paragraphing is attempted* but may run together or begin in the wrong places.

E. *Problems with grammar or usage are not serious* enough to distort meaning but may not be correct or accurately applied all of the time.

F. *Moderate* (a little of this, a little of that) *editing* would be required to polish the text for publication.

1 **Errors in spelling, punctuation, capitalization, usage and grammar, and/or paragraphing repeatedly distract the reader and make the text difficult to read. The writing reflects more than one of these problems:**

A. *Spelling errors are frequent,* even on common words.

B. *Punctuation* (including terminal punctuation) is often *missing or incorrect.*

C. *Capitalization* is *random,* and only the easiest rules show awareness of correct use.

D. *Errors in grammar or usage are very noticeable,* frequent, and affect meaning.

E. *Paragraphing is missing, irregular, or so frequent* (every sentence) that it has no relationship to the organizational structure of the text.

F. The reader must *read once to decode,* then again for meaning. *Extensive editing* (virtually every line) would be required to polish the text for publication.

SOURCE: © 2000, Northwest Regional Educational Laboratory, Portland, OR; 503-275-9500. Permission granted for use in the classroom.

CONVENTIONS
—*Editing*—

Readable to broad audience   *Punctuation smoothly guides reader*
Grammer contributes to clarity and style   **In control**   *"Clean copy"*
Paragraphing complements organization
Evidence of editing/proofing
Spelling mostly correct—even on harder words
Only light editing needed

Ready to share!

5

4

Halfway home!

Spelling correct on common words
Simple things done well
Paragraphing attempted

Problems don't obscure meaning
Writer occasionally "stumbles"
Errors consistent   *Minor problems in grammer/usage*
Hastily edited   *Terminal punctuation basically correct*

3

2

Just beginning

1

Tough to decide   *Numerous errors*   **Couldn't publish yet**
Little or no control over conventions
Paragraphing random or not present   **Struggling**
Readability impaired
Errors extremely distracting   **Cries out for editing**

PRESENTATION
(optional)

5 The form and presentation of the text enhances the ability for the reader to understand and connect with the message. It is pleasing to the eye.

A. If handwritten (either cursive or printed), the slant is consistent, letters are clearly formed, *spacing is uniform* between words, and the text is easy to read.

B. If word-processed, there is *appropriate use of fonts and font sizes* which invites the reader into the text.

C. The use of *white space* on the page (spacing, margins, etc.) allows the intended audience to easily focus on the text and message without distractions. There is just the right amount of balance of white space and text on the page. The formatting suits the purpose for writing.

D. The use of a *title, side heads, page numbering, bullets,* and evidence of correct use of a style sheet (when appropriate) makes it easy for the reader to access the desired information and text. These markers allow the hierarchy of information to be clear to the reader.

E. When appropriate to the purpose and audience, there is *effective integration of text and illustrations, charts, graphs, maps, tables, etc.* There is clear alignment between the text and visuals. The visuals support and clarify important information or key points made in the text.

3 The writer's message is understandable in this format.

A. *Handwriting is readable,* although there may be *discrepancies in letter shape and form, slant, and spacing* that may make some words or passages easier to read than others.

B. *Experimentation with fonts and font sizes* is successful in some places but begins to get fussy and cluttered in others. The *effect is not consistent* throughout the text.

C. While margins may be present, *some text may crowd the edges.* Consistent spacing is applied, although a different choice may make text more accessible (e.g. single, double, or triple spacing).

D. Although some markers are present (titles, numbering, bullets, side heads, etc.), they are not used to their fullest potential as a guide for the reader to access the greatest meaning from the text.

E. An *attempt is made to integrate visuals* and the text, although the connections may be limited.

1 The reader receives a garbled message due to problems relating to the presentation of the text.

A. Because the letters are irregularly slanted, formed inconsistently, or incorrectly, and the spacing is unbalanced or not even present, it is *very difficult to read and understand the text.*

B. The writer has gone *wild with multiple fonts and font sizes.* It is a major distraction to the reader.

C. The *spacing is random and confusing* to the reader. There may be little or no white space on the page.

D. *Lack of markers* (title, page numbering, bullets, side heads, etc.) leave the reader wondering how one section connects to another and why the text is organized in this manner on the page.

E. The visuals do not support or further illustrate key ideas presented in the text. They may be *misleading, indecipherable, or too complex* to be understood.

SOURCE: © 2000, Northwest Regional Educational Laboratory, Portland, OR; 503-275-9500. Permission granted for use in the classroom.

K-5 DEVELOPMENTAL WRITING SCALE

By the end of second grade, most children will enter the *Developing Writer Stage* (Step 8). In Grades 3, 4, and 5, children will progress within the *Developing Writer Stage*. By the end of the fifth grade, many children will be at the *Developing Writer Stage* (Step 10).

Prewriter Stage

Step 1 *Picture Writing*	*Step 2* *Scribble Writing*	*Step 3* *Mock Writing*	*Step 4* *Random Letter Writing*
PRODUCT CHARACTERISTICS • Message conveyed in the picture (precommunicative A spelling stage)	PRODUCT CHARACTERISTICS • Writing is represented as lines, scribbles, and scrawls or as a picture (precommunicative A spelling stage) • No recognizable letters • Writer can read the scribble but not over time • Writing can show knowledge of directionality	PRODUCT CHARACTERISTICS • Letter-like forms in imitation of writing • Often a mixture of real letters and/or drawings • Little or no sound/symbol relationships (precommunicative B spelling stage) • May be anywhere on the paper	PRODUCT CHARACTERISTICS • Letters begin to appear usually strung together, along with letter-like symbols • Contains more real letters • May show some sound/symbol relationships • A correctly spelled word may appear (precommunicative B spelling stage)
PROCESS CHARACTERISTICS • Talk revolves around the picture • Dictated message may convey a complete thought	PROCESS CHARACTERISTICS • Prewrite by drawing/interaction with teacher • Talk revolves around the picture • Access ideas expressed in their own writing through meaningful play experiences • Dictated message may convey complete thought	PROCESS CHARACTERISTICS • Prewrite by drawing/interaction with teacher • Talk revolves around the picture • Access ideas expressed in their own writing through meaningful play experiences • Dictated message may convey a complete thought	PROCESS CHARACTERISTICS • Prewrite by drawing/interaction with teacher • Talk revolves around the picture • Access ideas expressed in their own writing through meaningful play experiences • Dictated message may convey a complete thought

Emergent Writer Stage

By the end of second grade, most children will enter the *Developing Writer Stage* (Step 8). In Grades 3, 4, and 5, children will progress within the *Developing Writer Stage*. By the end of the fifth grade, many children will be at the *Developing Writer Stage* (Step 10).

Step 5 Writing Awareness	*Step 6* Stylized Sentence Writing	*Step 7* Conventional Writing
PRODUCT CHARACTERISTICS • Shows concept of letter and word • May or may not have spacing between words • May include sight words • Evidence of sound/symbol correspondence • Use of dominant consonants and some vowel sounds • Contains all real letters (semi-phonetic/phonetic spelling stage)	**PRODUCT CHARACTERISTICS** • Will stylize sentences around known words, repetitive phrases, and sentence beginnings • Uses words from the environment to complete sentences (phonetic/transitional spelling stage) • Message is predominantly contained in the writing • Writing now provides the clues which enable the message to be read over time	**PRODUCT CHARACTERISTICS** • Beginning to gain control of conventions of writing • Sentences are short, simple, and can be repetitious • Messages are little stories • Use both invented spelling and conventional spelling (transitional spelling stage)
PROCESS CHARACTERISTICS • Experiment with letter shapes to arrive at consistency of letter form • Often refer to environmental print • May begin to use a word processor to create text	**PROCESS CHARACTERISTICS** • Begin to show concern for the conventions of writing (i.e., spacing, capitalization, punctuation) • Begin to develop an awareness of their audience • Experiment with letter shapes to arrive at consistency of letter form • Often refer to environmental print • May begin to use a word processor to create text	**PROCESS CHARACTERISTICS** • Write freely, creatively, and independently • Taking more risks • Begin to edit • May begin to use a word processor to create text

SOURCE: © 1995, Wauwatosa, Wisconsin School District. Used with permission.

Emergent Writer Stage

By the end of second grade, most children will enter the *Developing Writer Stage* (Step 8). In Grades 3, 4, and 5, children will progress within the *Developing Writer Stage*. By the end of the fifth grade, many children will be at the *Developing Writer Stage* (Step 10).

Step 5 *Writing Awareness*	*Step 6* *Stylized Sentence Writing*	*Step 7* *Conventional Writing*[a]
		If I were in the Winter Olympics my sport would be bobsled I want to be in that sport because I like to go selding very fast I would practice going downhill in a big seld with three of my friends I would practice for 4 years I would go with three of my friends I would win a silver medal I would get in second place I would wear a siut with the Ameracin flag printed on it My firends and I will help and get a coach and get to the Olympics. When I was walking out of my house I saw two cars crash. The color of the car that crashed into the other car was black. And the color of the other car was red. When they crashed it made a bad bump sound.

Developing Writer Stage*

By the end of second grade, most children will enter the *Developing Writer Stage* (Step 8). In Grades 3, 4, and 5, children will progress within the *Developing Writer Stage*. By the end of the fifth grade, many children will be at the *Developing Writer Stage* (Step 10).

Step 8
Early Transitional

PRODUCT CHARACTERISTICS
- Begins to contain variation in sentence structure
- Stronger sense of voice emerges—at times can be wooden or inconsistent
- Story language and/or structure may be evident
- Reflects chronology of life's events, rather than a response to them
- Tends to be organized but may break down
- Length of text increases and may include less important information
- Tells everything that happens—doesn't weigh importance
- Sequenced and chronological
- Uses more conventions of writing (mechanics)
- Evidence of conventional spelling of high frequency words and more accurate use of vowel patterns (transitional spelling stage)

PROCESS CHARACTERISTICS
- Think they are finished too soon
- Preoccupation with correctness may restrict quality
- Begin to worry over topic
- Develop balance between content and mechanics
- Continue to edit and begin to revise
- Revisions tend to be corrections
- Initially choose giant topics
- Become more aware of the end product
- May begin to use a word processor to manipulate and publish text
- Broader writing episodes, encompassing looking ahead, looking back, anticipating, critiquing

Step 9
Mid Transitional

PRODUCT CHARACTERISTICS
- Organization is tightly structured, step-by-step
- Little use of transitions
- Sense of voice is more consistent
- Some things have more importance than others Beginning use of description is evident
- Beginning to select relevant details
- Uses conventions of writing more accurately
- More accurate use of conventional spelling patterns (transitional/conventional spelling stage)
- Uses more varied sentences

PROCESS CHARACTERISTICS
- May concentrate on one component of writing at a time
- Write for audience—believe writing is good if it's exciting, long, focused, full of sound effects, dialogue, and action
- Continue to edit and begin to revise
- Revisions tend to be corrections
- Initially choose giant topics
- Become more aware of the end product
- May begin to use a word processor to manipulate and publish text
- Broader writing episodes, encompassing looking ahead, looking back, anticipating, critiquing

Step 10
Late Transitional

PRODUCT CHARACTERISTICS
- Creative approach to interpretation of topic
- Sense of voice is evident
- Sense of audience is evident and consistent
- Accurate use of simple conventions of writing and spelling (conventional spelling stage)
- Includes descriptive language
- Includes interesting vocabulary
- May include paragraphing

PROCESS CHARACTERISTICS
- Additional risk-taking with complex conventions is noted
- Prewriting and drafting almost become one
- Can zoom ahead in mind's eye and return to organize and rearrange
- Gradually can think more things through before they write
- First drafts gradually become more detailed and fluent
- Develop and internalize strategies to make revisions
- Become more aware of the end product
- May begin to use a word processor to manipulate and publish text
- Broader writing episodes, encompassing looking ahead, looking back, anticipating critiquing

SOURCE: © 1995, Wauwatosa, Wisconsin School District. Used with permission.
Note: *This stage could last a long time and could include children of various ages.

Developing Writer Stage*

By the end of second grade, most children will enter the *Developing Writer Stage* (Step 8). In Grades 3, 4, and 5, children will progress within the *Developing Writer Stage*. By the end of the fifth grade, many children will be at the *Developing Writer Stage* (Step 10).

My weekend

Over the weekend I went to Madison. I went there to see a play. It was really good. It was called the Magic Chin's Nephew. I liked it a lot. Then we went to Michael's Custurd and brough custurd home for my Grandpa and Dad and Al. The play was the first of Narnia. It was about God our creater. Then I went up north. When we got in Parteeville there was 101 grage sales (I didn't count. I'm just being sarcastic.) There was grage sale after grage sale. We stoped at one but didn't get anything. When we got up north my cousin Annie asked if I wanted to go over to my Granny's old house. I said sure. She has a go cart and trampoleen. My cousin caught a cat fish like two feet long. We went on our boat. The go cart is not ours. It is my Uncle Tom. But we use it because we let him use our boat. We just got a boat lift for it. I didn't catch anything. My friend Ashely is in sixth grade. Her cabin is up the hill and down. She is going to sale her cabin. My Uncle Tom (a different one) wants to look at her cabin for a cabin. Well bye.

Step 8—Early Transitional

The Ameracen Egil ride

Once my mom and I went on the Amaracen Egil. We both sate in the sam car. When we were going up I started to get really scaerd. Then we got to the top and I was even more scaerd. Then we started going down, first slow and then fast. I told my mom I was really scaerd. She said, "It would not be very scaery. Then we were going really fast and I said, "I don't like this ride anymore." Then I held onto my mom because I thought I would fall out. I also held onto my Mom because the wind was blowing into my face and pushing me. I also held onto my mom because my stumik was feeling very sike when we stated going very fast.

A week ago my crayfish shed his x-o-scallaton and he got bigger. Not he is 2½ inches long. Sometimes when my fish go near my crayfish he snaps at them or he charges at them. My fish are about 2½ inches long, they are black. They have white dots on their forheads and one of my fish ownly has one fin on the side. I like my fish and my crayfish. My fish likes sleeping in groups on the left side. My cray fish likes sleeping in a house of rocks that we put in. My cray fish has shed his x-o-scallaton 2 times so far this year. They live in a fish bowl with a peble bottom. We clean the fish bowl every 3 weeks or every month. I caught my fish in a pond with a net.

The Missing Book

Last Friday I had a sleep over. I invited Natalie and Nicole. When we were getting in bed, Natalie said, "Can we read before we go to bed? "Sure," I said. So that night we read. The next morning Natalie got ready to go because she had to go at 8:00. We had breakfast and then the doorbell rang. It was Natalie's dad. I got Natalie's things and said "bye."

Then Nicole and me made a fort and we put our books in our sleeping bags. Then it was noon so we had to take Nicole home.

The next day I was looking for my book. I couldn't find it anywhere. Four days latter I was still looking for it. Then I said, "Maybe it's in my sleeping bag." So I looked and there it was my book. I raced downstairs and told my Dad. He was so happy I found it. And then I started to reading it.

My Cousins Football Game

One day I came home from school my mother asked me if I wanted to go to my cousin's football game. I said I would so she dropped me off over my aunt's house. From there we went to the football game. It was a huge stadiam. The game had already started. My cousin's team was looseing. The name of my cousin's team is the wildcats. The other team is tech. My cousin's team lost 20-0. A few days later he said his side hurt. He had to stay in bed because he was sick after that. I never heard of him playing football again.

Developing Writer Stage*

Step 9—Mid Transitional

SANTA CLAUSE

Once there was a man who lived in a log cabin in the North Pole. The man always stayed in his cabin except when he needed supplies like wood for fires and building, paint to paint the things he built, and food for him and his wife to eat and cook with. The man and his wife were a little chubby. In winter their cheeks were as red as roses. The man always wore trowsers and knit pants. His wife wore dresses. All of the clothes they wore were red, white, and green. One day the sky got very dark. Over night there was a snowstorm. When the man woke up he looked out the window and saw all the snow on the ground. He was so excited that he yelled out to his wife. "There's about 2 feet of snow on the ground." When the man's wife heard her husband yell she hopped out of bed and ran into the family room where she found her husband jumping up and down. "I know that you love it when it snows but you're going to have to calm down." Well it just so happened that almost everyone that lived in the North Pole knew that the man loved snow. A little boy named Sam Tomson who was 5 years old wanted to know if the man was excited so he walked in 2 feet of snow up the mountain to the man and his wife's house. When he got in the man's house he knocked on the door. He wondered what the man and his wife looked like. Just then the door swung open. At the door was the man and his wife. The man had a white beard and white hair. He was about 5 feet tall. (The size of an elf.) The man's wife had grey hair and was about 5 feet tall also. The first thing he said was, "Hi, do you want to go on a walk with me?" "Sure," said the old man So the old man got his winter coat on. Then they went on a walk. When they were on the walk they talked about the snowstorm. "I love snow!" said the old man.

"Me to!" said Sam. Just then the man heard something. The man turned around and saw 8 reindeer. "My reindeer!" the man shouted. "I found my 8 reindeer that I lost last Christmas!"

The Wierd Guy

It all started like a normal day. Then the clouds started moving in. My friend and I decided to go on a bike ride. We started out on our street and went by Subway. Then we went by the movie store and past Pius Xi. We turned around and went the other way. We just got on Glenview Road when this brown car started following us.

We went threw St. Jude but he was waiting right where we got out. We started back to my house but he followed us. We went down Blue Mound R.D. but he still followed us.

We turned on Honey Creek Road and we saw him start to pull something out of a bag. He put it in when the car came by. He turned to go back on are street. We had to bike up a step hill. He almost crashed into us but we moved over way to the side. We got up and started for my house. We

The Road Trip to Florida

We left our house at 5:00 p.m. and my family hoped to reach Florida by the next night. As we were crossing the border between Wisconsin and Illinois I heard the clang, clang of the money going into the toll booth. Then I thought to myself this is going to be a long trip. It's 8:30 right now and everybody is yelling and screaming. I wish we could just turn around. Julie turned around and said to me.

"Look what the sign says. It says we're already in Indianapolis."

"Cool," I said with excitement . . . Now it's 10:30 and 2 hours have gone by and Mom and Sarah are sleeping but I am keeping Dad company. I think Brian is going to be the only one keeping Dad company pretty soon. It's 6:15 a.m. and we're somewhere in Tennessee and the sunrise is beautiful.

Everything is a golden yellow orange color. Now Mom is stirring because Dad definitely needs a rest.

(continued)

SOURCE: © 1995, Wauwatosa, Wisconsin School District. Used with permission.
Note: *This stage could last a long time and could include children of various ages.

The Wierd Guy (continued)

were going as fast as we could. We just got to my drive way and he stoped. He watched us until we got inside. I have never seen him or his car since.

SANTA CLAUSE (continued)

"Do you want to take your reindeer home" asked Sam.

"Sure!" said the old man. So the old men and Sam took the reindeer to the old man's house. When the old men and Sam got to the old man's house the old man put his 8 reindeer in a barn he had in his backyard. After he did that he went back out to his front yard to say good bye to Sam. In the man's front yard Sam was waiting for the old man to come back. When the man came back Sam said, "I'm sorry but I have to go home to eat lunch." "OK," said the old man and waved good bye. Sam waved back. Then the man opened the door and went inside. Sam was just about to leave but he saw a sign on the old man's door. The sign said SANTA'S WORK SHOP. Sam was so excited that he ran home as fast as he could. He couldn't wait to tell his mom, his dad, his 2 brothers, and his 3 sisters. When Sam got home he ran all over his house yelling, "Hey everybody, I know where Santa lives." Just then Sam's mother saw Sam running all over the house. "What are you doing Sam? You know that your not allowed to run in the house the night before Christmas Eve when we are having the Christmas party. You might break something." said Sam's mother.

"Sorry," said Sam. Just then Sam's sister Sara yelled, "What's going on in here" Sam was running around the kitchen table when Sara and Sam's 2 older brothers Mike and Dan and his other 2 sisters Lindsay and Emily came running into the kitchen. Sam had to stop to catch his breath, then he said, "I know where Santa lives!"

"How do you know where he lives"? asked Emily.

"Because I went up the mountain to tell the old man how much it snowed an on his door there was a sign that said SANTA'S WORKSHOP on it."

"Does he have any reindeer?" Sara asked.

"Yes he does and he has exactly 8," Sam said.

"Well you better show him to us some time or we won't believe you" said Sara.

The Road Trip to Florida (continued)

___ just woke up and the first person he is waking up is ___. Lucky her, I thought to myself sarcastically.

"Can I wake up Dad, it's 9:00?" I said

"No, just calm down. Dad needs his rest," said Mom. At 11:30 we finally stopped because everybody was sick of sitting around in the van.

"We're already in Atlanta," I said with excitement. We jumped back in the car and hit the road. . . .

My mom called her family. . .

"Wow what a trip." I'm wiped out. As we went to bed. . .

"No I can't!" Sam said.

"Why can't you?" Mike said in a mean tone.

"Because!" Sam said back to him.

"Children stop fighting and get upstairs and get ready for the party."

So the children went upstairs and got ready. When all the children were ready they sat down and told each other what they wanted for Christmas. When they all told each other what they wanted they went downstairs. When they got downstairs they noticed everyone was there.

"Wash up for dinner," their mother said. So the children went to wash their hands. When they came back to the table everyone was already eating dinner. The children went and got their plates and dished themselves up. Then they had dinner with everyone else. After everyone was done and all the plates were washed and put away, everyone went into the living room to exchange gifts. After all the gifts were passed out the children went upstairs and got in their beds. During the night Santa came to everyone in the world. In the morning they opened their presents from Santa. They all got neat presents and after that even Sara believed Sam saw the real Santa. THE END.

SOURCE: © 1995, Wauwatosa, Wisconsin School District. Used with permission.
Note: *This stage could last a long time and could include children of various ages.

Developing Writer Stage*

By the end of second grade, most children will enter the *Developing Writer Stage* (Step 8). In Grades 3, 4, and 5, children will progress within the *Developing Writer Stage*. By the end of the fifth grade, many children will be at the *Developing Writer Stage* (Step 10).

Step 10—Late Transitional

Tiger

My cat is Tiger Manders. Tiger is big. He has orange fur with brownish stripes. He also has large eyes that turn yellow and glow in the dark. He is a tabby cat, though he doesn't act like one. About the only characteristics that are the same are inherited. He must get all his other things from environment. Unlike most tabbies Tiger isn't afraid of water, other cats, dogs, raccoons, unfamiliar people, and other dangers. Tiger is strong and can jump high, climb trees, and climb our house without front claws.

My cat can be very mean. He got in a fight with a raccoon once. We were scared Tiger might get hurt. We only heard sounds but we knew it was Tiger.

"Tiger!" we yelled.

"Maaaaaareowl" he seemed to answer in a plea. It was only for a short while but it seemed like years. All of a sudden the noise stopped.

Tiger walked up.

One day my dad and I went up in an airplane with two parachutes and were going to attempt the most high jump in the history of America. We had been training for this jump for over 3 years now. If one little thing went wrong, we would just be one greesy spot in the road. We were so high that we couldn't see the ground, only because the clouds were thick that day. We were about to jump so we double checked our gear and on 10 we would jump. 10, 9, 8, 7, 6, 5, 4, 3, 2, 1. ahhhhh!!! The sensation of flying like a bird was the best feeling I ever had. I was just floating for about 3 minutes when I realised it was time to open my shoot. So I reached back to pull the cord and waited for it to come out...It didn't. I pulled it again and again and it still did not open. I was scared out of my mind that I was going to be flat in about 1 minute. I would just be a greesy spot in the road. I tried to reach back for the emergency shoot but the force of the wind was to strong. I could see the ground very clearly now. I got closer and closer and started to yell and screme and all of a sudden I landed with a big thump. I could not believe I was alive. I opened my eyes and....

I saw my bed to the right of me. Then I felt my cat come and lick my face. I was thinking that I had died and gone to heaven. But when I saw my mom come in and say, "Time for breakfast, what do you want." Then I realised that I was just having a bad dream, a night mare, and I didn't really jump out of a plane and the shoot didn't open. I had just fallen out of my bed.

THE ENORMOUS EGG

Once upon a time about a few years ago, there lived a boy named Tim and his pa. They dwelled together on a big farm in Wisconsin.

The farm had lots of animals, chickens, roosters, horses, pigs, and even a little barnyard kitten.

Early every spring morning, Tim gathered the eggs from the chickens and some days he left an egg or two for a chicken to hatch.

On morning when Tim was gathering eggs, he found an ENORMOUS egg! It was as big as the WHOLE nest and the nest was pretty big!

"Pa" called Tim, "Pa, come look what I found! It's a HUGE egg! Hurry up!" Pa dashed to the barn calling, "Where is it. Where is it?"

Tim darted back into the house and woke Pa.

"Pa" called Tim, "Pa, come look what I found! It's a HUGE egg! Hurry up!" Pa dashed to the barn calling, "Where is it. Where is it?"

When they both arrived at the barn Jim called, "It's right over here! Look how big it is!"

Pa arrived at the next, "Yup that's a big one."

"It's not just big it's HUGE!" Tim replied.

It was about easter now. Tim and Pa were hanging up decorations. Pa asked curiously "Has that egg hatched yet?"

"No, Pa, not yet," Tim answered.

"It's been a month so far and that egg hasn't hatched yet."

Tim replied, "I wonder when it's going to hatch."

At supper Tim was all worked up because dinner was the next day.

"Pa, Pa easter's tomorrow!" Tim shouted. "I can't wait!"

Well you better settle down and get to bed or the easter Bunny won't come," Pa said.

"Good night, Pa," said Tim.

"Good night," said Pa.

Tim dawdled slowly up to bed. He was too excited to sleep but some how he drifted off.

In the morning darted downstairs. He ran outside to get the eggs. When Tim checked in on the big egg it had a crack in it.

Tim ran to tell Pa the news. "Pa, the egg has a crack in it!" Pa came rushing to the barn wearing his robe and pajamas.

Pa arrived at the nest. The egg had hatched. Inside the egg were lots of tiny chocolate eggs covered in tin foil.

"What happened to you?' someone questioned knowing he wouldn't get an answer. Tiger's fur was sticking straight up. He wanted to go inside immediately. Tiger ran in and ate.

He turned out not being hurt at all. In all the fight's Tiger has gotten in it has turned out the same. Tiger always seems to come out on top. I hope it stays that way forever.

A Day At The Ponds

Yesterday, November 10th, my class went to the ponds. Mike, Brian, and I went to make a fort in a tree, near the ponds. There are already some boobie traps there like we were wipped by branches on the tree. When we got there, we looked for that very tree and we climb up it and saw a rabbit bound away. It was very cool! One glimps of that rabbit and I felt like it was a bolt of lighning, flashing by twisting and turning. Then I saw it bound away from Steve and Eric. I couldn't believe my eyes. Jim also saw it and he seemed like it had never happened to him before. We were all astounded by how it dashes away from a preditor. . .it was the neatest sight I ever saw!

SOURCE: © 1995, Wauwatosa, Wisconsin School District. Used with permission.

Note: *This stage could last a long time and could include children of various ages.

Independent Writer Stage*

By the end of second grade, most children will enter the *Developing Writer Stage* (Step 8). In Grades 3, 4, and 5, children will progress within the *Developing Writer Stage*. By the end of the fifth grade, many children will be at the *Developing Writer Stage* (Step 10).

PRODUCT CHARACTERISTICS

- Strong sense of voice
- Strong sense of audience
- Well developed
- Includes supportive details
- Sentences are correct and varied to create interest
- The message creates impact and evokes the desired response and/or further thinking from the reader
- Accurate use of simple and more complex conventions of writing, including introduction, conclusion, paragraphing (conventional spelling stage)
- Includes rich, descriptive language
- May include more than one point of view
- Realizes that the audience expects to see a correct script

PRODUCT CHARACTERISTICS

- Internalize questions good writers ask themselves
- Has internalized the process

Step 11—Independent Writing

She, the Adventuress

"Good-bye! We will miss you!" Angela Pine called out to her 17 year old daughter, Anita. "Oohh! Oohh!" sounded the ship's whistle. The ship was leaving.

Anita Pine was an only child and smart for her age. She like adventures and that's why she was going on this trip ALONE.

The best was going to the Island of Pyzihohy. This was Anita's first trip alone.

"How do you like the ride so far, Miss Pine?" asked the captain.

"Very nice," answered Anita.

A man in a sailor suit came along.

"Hi Tim," said the captain. "Miss Pine, this is Tim, He is my first mate."

"Pleased to meet you, Ma'am," Tim told Anita.

Anita blushed.

"Take her bags, will you?" asked the captain.

"Yes Sir!"

Anita followed Tim to her cabin on the ship. She opened the door with her key.

"Thanks," she said. "I'm going to turn in." She closed the door.

That night Anita was sleeping very peacefully until she heard a big, thundering crash that came from the deck. Anita grabbed her pants and a sweater, put them on, opened the door, walked outside, locked her cabin, and ran.

When Anita stepped on the deck she almost fell into the pool. The captain was out on the deck in his pajamas with his daughter, Lou. There were boxes scattered everywhere. There were thirteen to be exact.

"Tim!" called the captain. "Get on the deck right now!"

Tim came in his robe. "Why Sir, why did you do this?"

"I didn't do it! Do you think I'd want to do this?"

"No Sir!"

"Captain, Tim, what's the need for arguing? What we've go to do is found out who did it?" said Anita.

Now before I go on, there is one thing I should tell you. Anita Pine LOVES mysteries. In fact, some people call her Private Eye Pine!

While Tim, Anita, the captain, and Lou were picking up the bones, a lady came out screaming.

Life's Mystery

So swiftly she moved, her pale feet, brushing gently across the silken meadows. She drifted, as if soaring through the clean fresh air, on a sparrow's wing. But she wasn't. She was not floating but falling, plunging to her death. I ran to save her but it was too late. She hit the ground and then her eyes closed. The birds stopped singing and the leaves stopped falling. It wasn't the same without her. She was a goddess to everyone and brought spring, summer, and fall. Only one season did she not bring. The evil winter. He killed her for revenge. For she was beautiful and he was ugly. She brought happy times and he brought times of anger and famine, disease and hate. Everyone loved her, everyone hated him. He made her fall, but how could someone so good die? Now everyone must love him, and thank him for the seasons of good. But when he had all the seasons in his power, nothing seemed to be good anymore. People hated each other, and killed, and fought wars. This was the way he liked it. No person was happy with what they got. It was now a world of greed, and plague. People stole and polluted. There was only one peaceful place. That was where She was buried. Four people spent their lives there, worshipping her. They could not be touched by the evil one. Around them they could not see the bad things that were going on. They did not want to look either. The evil one had gained so much power that whole countries suffered, and people had to build jails and courthouses. There were many for miles around. Too much crime was going on. Was there a way to stop it? Was there a way to stop the pollution? The people were getting desperate. The earth was getting too crowded. What were we to do? It all depended on the children. Could they change what has happened to the world? Maybe. But maybe not. If you want to know, I can't tell you the answer.

"I just saw a dark figure go pass my window," said lady. "My name is Shirley Burge."

"Miss . . ." started Anita.

"Mrs."

"Oh yeah, Mrs. Burge. Come on! Let's find the dude! Don't worry." Anita said as she grabbed Mrs. Burge's hand.

"Really some kid, isn't she Captain?" asked Tim.

"I guess."

"First, let's inspect your area and window," Anita said.

"Why the window?" inquired Mrs. Burge.

"Just in case the window was playing tricks on you."

They looked for prints, too.

"I found some!" screamed Mrs. Burge suddenly. Lights went on aboard the ship. A lot of "shh" and "Can't you se some of us are trying to sleep?" were heard.

"Never mind them," Anita told Mrs. Burge. "Where do they lead to?"

"Well let's see—right here! Agh!"

There was a man standing at the end of the tracks. "Got you!" shouted Anita. Lights went on again. "Shut up!" shouted a man.

"Back to you!" yelled Mrs. Burge.

Anita grabbed a fishing net and threw it over the man's head.

"Why, you're just a kid!" yelled the man in a voice that knifed across to the deck. The captain, Tim, and Lou came running.

"You've caught him!" said the amazed First Mate.

"Yes she has," grunted the man. Some gold coins fell out of the man's pocket. "You're the one who stole them!" shouted the captain. "We'll put you in jail. These are the ship's."

The next three days were boring when compared to the first night. That is, all except for the last night. There was a big dance. Anita danced with Tim the whole night. The days on the island were hot, but not too to ruin Anita's fun. Anita had fun. She went shopping also. She went to the beach every day.

On the plan ride home to Poway (San Diego) Anita had lobster and potatoes. (A VERY delicious meal.)

When Anita got home everyone greeted her with a warm welcome. "I missed you all," said Anita and began telling them her adventures.

THE END

SOURCE: © 1995, Wauwatosa, Wisconsin School District. Used with permission.
Note: *This stage could last a long time and could include children of various ages.

Independent Writer Stage*

By the end of second grade, most children will enter the *Developing Writer Stage* (Step 8). In Grades 3, 4, and 5, children will progress within the *Developing Writer Stage*. By the end of the fifth grade, many children will be at the *Developing Writer Stage* (Step 10).

Step 11—Independent Writing

"Hi Mom! I'm home!" cried David Caliron. "Wow! What's that?"

"It's a plant that I bought at the plant store. Do you like the big flower on it?" asked Mrs. Caliron.

"Yes! It's beautiful!" exclaimed David.

"Hi, Mom!" said Nancy Caliron as she came into the room. "Wow! What a beautiful plant!"

"Mom got it at the plant store," said David.

"It sure is pretty. What kind of plant is it?" asked Nancy.

"I asked the florist, but he didn't know. He said he had bought it from a horticulturist who didn't say what kind of plant it was."

"What's a horticulturist?" asked David.

"A horticulturist is someone who grows plants and sells them to a florist," answered Mrs. Caliron. "But enough about plants. Come and eat your snack." So Nancy and David forgot all about the plant.

The next morning Nancy noticed that there was a lot more dirt in the plant's pot.

"Mom, wasn't there enough dirt in the plant's pot before?" Nancy asked Mrs. Caliron.

"I didn't put any dirt in the plant's pot," Mrs. Caliron replied. Just then David called from the kitchen,

"Mom, I thought it was my job to take out the garbage!"

"It is your job." Said Mrs. Caliron.

"Then why isn't there any garbage in the garbage can?"

"I don't know. I didn't take out the garbage. Did you take out the garbage Nancy?" Mrs. Caliron asked.

"No," said Nancy and before David could say anything else, she asked him, "Why did you put more dirt in the plant's pat?"

"I didn't put any more dirt in the plant's pot," David said.

"Wait a minute," Mrs. Caliron said. "If none of us took out the garbage, and none of us put more dirt in the plant's pot, who did?"

"A burglar?" Nancy whispered.

"Of course not, silly," David said. "Burglers don't go around taking out the garbage and filling plants' pots with dirt!" "I know!" cried Nancy. The plant ate the garbage and turned it into dirt."

"Yeah!" said David.

"That's ridiculous!" said Mrs. Caliron. But the next day the garbage was gone and there was more dirt in the pot.

"Kids, if it's true that this plant eats garbage we could make more of them and with a lot more of them the world would be a much better place," Mrs. Caliron exclaimed.

"But how do we make more of them?" David asked.

"With seeds in that flower," Mrs. Clairon said. In a few weeks, the seeds that David, Nancy and Mrs. Caliron had planted had grown very big. Then Mrs. Caliron took half of them to the plant store, after taking the seeds out of the flowers. That way, people would buy them and take them home and the plants would eat their garbage.

"What are you going to do with the other half, Mom?" Nancy asked.

"You will see," Mrs. Caliron answered.

When she got back home, Mrs. Caliron told David and Nancy what they woul do with the other half of their plants.

"We will plant these plants outside all over the place! The plants will spread their seeds and make more plants! Whenever someone litters, the plants will eat it up!" Mrs. Caliron exclaimed. "We could put them in landfills too," said David.

Well, after a while people had realized that this kind of plant ate garbage. Nancy, David, and Mrs. Caliron were famous and the world was free of garbage.

THE END

156

SOURCE: © 1995, Wauwatosa, Wisconsin School District. Used with permission.
Note: *This stage could last a long time and could include children of various ages.

GROUP DISCUSSION RUBRIC

This is a composite rubric synthesized from several sources. It is not meant to be a checklist—the descriptors under each level of performance are indicators of the quality of performance rather than an exhaustive listing; not everything must be "checked off" to receive a score of a particular level. The rubric should be considered a work in progress. (*Note:* The article by David Harris cited in the footnote provides sample dialogues that illustrate many of the indicators in the rubric.)

Trait 1: Content Understanding—comprehension of the content under discussion

High

➡ The student understands significant ideas relevant to the issue under discussion. This is indicated by correct use of terminology, precise selection of the pieces of information required to make a point, correct and appropriate use of examples and counterexamples, demonstration of which distinctions are important to make, and explanations that are concise and to the point.

➡ Information and knowledge are accurate.

➡ The student elaborates statements with accurate explanations, reasons, or evidence.

Medium

➡ Ideas are reasonably clear, but the listener needs to make some guesses as to what the student meant.

➡ Some vocabulary is used correctly and some is not.

➡ Ideas are correct but not concise.

➡ Contributions to the group are generally supported by some facts, examples, analogies, statistics, and so forth, but there's a sense that more is needed.

Low

➡ The student uses foundational knowledge incorrectly.

➡ The student struggles to provide ideas or support for ideas.

➡ Ideas are extremely limited or hard to understand.

➡ The student has difficulty understanding themes and distinguishing main ideas and supporting details.

➡ Terminology is used incorrectly.

SOURCE: © 1999 Assessment Training Institute, Portland, OR, 503-228-3060; used with permission.

Trait 2: Reasoning—ability to use the content to explore an issue, reach agreement, make a decision, or discuss a point

High

➡ The student actively participates in the development of the group mission.

➡ The student states and identifies relevant subordinate issues. These can be ethical ("Should we make a value judgment of what is right or wrong?"), definitional ("Are we all using this word in the same manner?"), or factual ("What evidence do we have for this claim?"). There is deliberate and systematic consideration of embedded and related issues.

➡ The student takes a position or makes a claim and defends it with explanations, reasons, or evidence.

➡ The student stipulates claims or definitions (e.g., "For our discussion, let's agree that conduct refers to behavior while on military duty or while off duty but in uniform"). The student realizes when such stipulations are needed.

➡ The student recognizes values or value conflict as things that form the assumption basis of arguments and recognizes when it is important to acknowledge these values.

➡ The student argues by analogy.

➡ The student recognizes the accuracy, logic, relevance, or clarity of statements. The student recognizes contradictions and irrelevant comments.

➡ The student has a clear idea of the shape of the task and sustains inquiry until the task is completed. The student knows when the task is completed satisfactorily.

➡ The student asks clarifying questions and knows when clarifying questions need to be asked.

➡ The student distinguishes fact from opinion.

➡ The student summarizes points of agreement and disagreement to set the stage for further movement; the student knows when such summaries are useful.

Medium

➡ The student relies on the momentum of the group to motivate inquiry.

➡ The student generally distinguishes fact from opinions.

➡ The student may be repetitive with comments.

Low

➡ The student accepts ideas of others without much thought.

➡ The student jumps randomly from one aspect of an issue to another.

➡ The student provides little relevant information or contributes little to the discussion.

➡ Opinions may be stated as facts.

➡ The student shows little evidence of understanding the task and how to sustain the inquiry to adequately fulfill it.

➡ There is little sense of which information is of most importance.

➡ The student frequently asks for repetition of ideas but shows little evidence of understanding.

SOURCE: © 1999 Assessment Training Institute, Portland, OR, 503-228-3060; used with permission.

Trait 3: Interaction With Others

High

➡ The student initiates the development of the group process including identifying roles and accepting responsibility for fulfilling assigned roles within the group.

➡ Interaction reflects group norms—the student is appropriate for the group and setting.

➡ The student invites contributions from others as needed and the student knows when such contributions are needed.

➡ The student acknowledges the statements of others in a way that builds a consecutive interchange between participants.

➡ Replies to others are responsive to the statement and indicate that the student understood it and thought about it.

➡ When disagreeing, the student does it respectfully. The nature of the disagreement is stated and an invitation to respond extended.

➡ The student makes sure that all relevant points of view are heard.

➡ The student is courteous and attentive.

➡ Nonverbal behavior is consistent with verbal behavior; both are positive. Positive nonverbal behavior includes nodding, learning forward, and maintaining eye contact.

➡ The student is aware of cultural differences in social interactions and behaves in an appropriate fashion.

➡ When conflicts arise, the student attempts to resolve them.

➡ Talking is task-oriented and group-oriented—"we."

➡ Decision making is shared; there is lots of evidence of teaming and collaboration.

Medium

➡ The student participates in the development of the group process including identifying roles and accepting responsibility for fulfilling assigned roles within the group.

➡ The student attends to the discussion but doesn't participate very much.

➡ The student's contributions do not detract from the group's purpose or goals.

➡ The student participates in the group with prompting.

➡ The student responds to solicitation of opinions or ideas but doesn't volunteer them.

Low

➡ The student does not fulfill assigned roles.

➡ Interaction does not reflect group norms.

➡ The student makes irrelevant or distracting statements.

➡ Interruptions, when they occur, are unconstructive and noncourteous.

➡ The student monopolizes the conversation—a pattern of domination with the effect of preventing others from contributing.

SOURCE: © 1999 Assessment Training Institute, Portland, OR, 503-228-3060; used with permission.

➡ The student makes a personal attack; language might suggest bias toward a group member or others.

➡ The student is uninvolved in the discussion, even when directly asked for an opinion.

➡ Nonverbal behavior is inconsistent with verbal behavior—usually the nonverbal behavior is very negative while the verbal behavior might be positive. Nonverbal behavior may alienate the student from other group members.

➡ The student appears unaware of cultural differences in conducting discussions.

➡ Talk is self-oriented—"I."

➡ Work is done by individuals; there is little attempt at teaming or collaboration.

Trait 4: Language

High

➡ The student uses precise vocabulary and economical syntax. Words and syntax are purposefully chosen to make a point.

➡ The student uses language that others in the group will understand.

➡ The student defines or clearly explains language or concepts that might be unfamiliar to others; the student knows when such explanations might be necessary.

Medium

➡ The student uses general vocabulary and tends to express ideas wordily.

➡ Although correct, language might not be equally understandable to all members of the group.

Low

➡ The student uses language that others in the group are unlikely to understand.

➡ Ideas appear disproportionately lengthy and are difficult to follow.

➡ Language choices are vague, abstract, or trite. Jargon may be used when more precise language is needed.

SOURCE: © 1999, Assessment Training Institute, Portland, OR; 503-228-3060. Used with permission. Condensed from: (1) David Harris, *Assessing Discussion of Public Issues: A Scoring Guide*, in Ronald Evans and David Warren Saxe (Eds.) *Handbook on Teaching Social Issues*, NCSS Bulletin 93, 1996; (2) Alberta Education, *Oral Communication Evaluation: English 30/33 Activities and Scoring Guides*, Learning Resources Distributing Center, 12360 142nd St., Edmonton, Alberta T5L 4X9, 1992; (3) John Zola, *Scored Discussions, Social Education*, February 1992, pp. 121-125; (4) *History-Social Science, Grade 11*, California Learning Assessment System, California Department of Education, P.O. Box 944272, Sacramento, California 94244; (5) Paula Usrey, Group Discussion Member Rubric, NWREL, 503-275-9500, 1998; (6) Kansas State Department of Education, *State Assessment—Social Studies*, 1995; (7) Oregon Department of Education, *Collaborate Scoring Guide*, July 1994.

GENERAL CONCEPTUAL UNDERSTANDING RUBRIC

Conceptual understanding is the extent to which students understand the content to be learned.

High: A high score in conceptual understanding means that the student shows an accurate and extensive understanding of the topic. This can be shown in many ways, including:

➡ Correct and precise use of terminology

➡ Precise selection of the pieces of information required to make a point (no more, no less)

➡ Correct and appropriate use of examples and counterexamples

➡ Few errors in information

➡ Connections made to other, related topics

➡ Demonstration of which distinctions are important to make

➡ Key concepts identified and addressed

➡ A relevant focus sustained throughout the work

➡ Relevant use of a diagram or graph; knows when such things will aid understanding

➡ Concise explanations that are to the point

Medium: A medium score in conceptual understanding means that the student presents some important information, but there is a sense that the student is only about halfway home in terms of understanding. Performance is indicated by:

➡ Reasonably clear ideas, but the readers needs to make some guesses as to what the student meant

➡ Even though a general point is made, the student hasn't fine-tuned the topic

➡ Some parts of the work seem repetitive

➡ The balance in the work seems a little off

➡ Some vocabulary is used well, some is not

➡ Some examples and graphics are appropriate, some aren't

➡ Sometimes the student seems to know which concepts and points are most important and telling; other times not

➡ Information seems to be based on retelling rather than the student making his or her own connections

➡ The focus tends to shift

Low: A low score in conceptual understanding indicates that the student is still searching for the connections that will make the content meaningful. Weak performance is indicated by such things as:

➠ Ideas are extremely limited or hard to understand, even when the reader tries to draw inferences based on what is there

➠ The text may be repetitious or read like a collection of disconnected, random thoughts

➠ Information is inaccurate

➠ Terminology is used incorrectly

➠ There is little sense of which information is most important

➠ Visual displays, when used, are not helpful or unrelated to any points the student is trying to make

---

ON-DEMAND SPEAKING

Content

The content rating focuses on the specific things which are said. It is concerned with the amount of content related to the task, the relevance of the content to the task and the adaptation of the content to the listener and the situation.

1 = The delivery is **inadequate** in meeting the requirements of the task.
- The speaker says practically nothing.
- The speaker focuses primarily on irrelevant content.
- The speaker is highly egocentric. The speaker appears to ignore the listener and the situation.

2 = The content is **minimal** in meeting the requirements of the task.
- The speaker does not provide enough content to meet the requirements of the task.
- The speaker includes some irrelevant content. The speaker wanders off the topic.
- The speaker adapts poorly to the listener and the situation. The speaker uses words and concepts which are inappropriate for the knowledge and experiences of the listener (e.g., slang, jargon, technical language). The speaker uses arguments which are self-centered rather than other-centered.

3 = The delivery is **adequate** in meeting the requirements of the task.
- The speaker provides enough content to meet the requirements of the task.
- The speaker focuses primarily on relevant content. The speaker sticks to the topic.
- The speaker adapts the content in a general way to the listener and the situation. The speaker uses words and concepts which are appropriate for the knowledge and experience of a general audience. The speaker uses arguments which are adapted to a general audience.

4 = The delivery is **superior** in meeting the requirements of the task. Examples are:
- The speaker provides a variety of types of content appropriate for the task, such as generalizations, details, examples, and various forms of evidence.

SOURCE: © 1983, Massachusetts Department of Education. Reprinted with permission from *Development of the State Speaking Assessment Instrument: Reliability and Feasibility Study, 1983* and *Reliability and Feasibility Study, 1982*, State of Massachusetts, Department of Education, 350 Main Street, Malden, Massachusetts 02148.

■ The speaker adapts the content in a specific way to the listener and situation. The speaker takes into account the specific knowledge and experience of the listener, adds explanations as necessary, and refers to the listener's experience. The speaker uses arguments which are adapted to the values and motivations of the specific listener.

NOTE: This rating is concerned with content in terms of quantity, relevance, and adaptation. It is not concerned with content in terms of accuracy. Concerns with accuracy of content fall outside a speaking skills assessment. Also, make sure you are not unconsciously "filling in" content for a speaker because you happen to know something about the speaker's topic. If you add information, this fact should be reflected in your rating. REMEMBER, in this component you are rating the quantity, relevance, and adaptation of what the student says, not the accuracy of what the student says.

SOURCE: © 1983, Massachusetts Department of Education. Reprinted with permission from *Development of the State Speaking Assessment Instrument: Reliability and Feasibility Study, 1983* and *Reliability and Feasibility Study, 1982*, State of Massachusetts, Department of Education, 350 Main Street, Malden, Massachusetts 02148.

ORGANIZATION

The organization rating focuses on how the content of the message is structured. It is concerned with sequence and the relationships among the ideas in the message.

1 = The organization is **inadequate** in meeting the requirements of the task. Examples are:

- The message is so disorganized that you cannot understand most of the message.

2 = The organization is **minimal** in meeting the requirements of the task. Examples are:

- The organization of the message is mixed up; it jumps back and forth.
- The organization of the message appears random or rambling.
- You have difficulty understanding the sequence and relationships among the ideas in the message. You have to make some assumptions about the sequence and relationships of ideas.
- You cannot put the ideas in the message into an outline.

3 = The organization is **adequate** in meeting the requirements of the task. Examples are:

- The message is organized.
- You do not have difficulty understanding the sequence and relationships among the ideas in the message. You do not have to make assumptions about the sequence and relationships of ideas.
- You can put the ideas in the message into an outline.

4 = The organization is **superior** in meeting the requirements of the task. Examples are:

- The message is overtly organized.
- The speaker helps you understand the sequence and relationships of ideas by using organizational aids such as announcing the topic, previewing the organization, using transitions, and summarizing.

NOTE: Make sure you are not unconsciously "filling in" organization for a speaker, because you happen to know something about the speaker's topic. If you have to make assumptions about the organization, this fact should be reflected in your rating. REMEMBER, in this component you are rating how the student organizes the message, not what the student says.

SOURCE: © 1983, Massachusetts Department of Education. Reprinted with permission from *Development of the State Speaking Assessment Instrument: Reliability and Feasibility Study, 1983* and *Reliability and Feasibility Study, 1982,* State of Massachusetts, Department of Education, 350 Main Street, Malden, Massachusetts 02148.

DELIVERY

The delivery rating focuses on the transmission of the message. It is concerned with *volume, rate,* and *articulation.* Articulation refers to pronunciation and enunciation. Some examples of poor articulation include mumbling, slurring words, stammering, stuttering, and exhibiting disfluencies such as "ahs," "uhms," or "you knows."

1 = The delivery is **inadequate** in meeting the requirements of the task. Examples are:

- The volume is so low that you cannot understand most of the message.
- The rate is so fast that you cannot understand most of the message.
- The pronunciation and enunciation are so unclear that you cannot understand most of the message.

2 = The delivery is **minimal** in meeting the requirements of the task. Examples are:

- The volume is too low or too loud.
- The rate is too fast or too slow. Pauses are too long or at inappropriate spots.
- The pronunciation and enunciation are unclear. The speaker exhibits many disfluencies, such as "ahs," "umhs," or "you knows."
- You are distracted by problems in the delivery of the message.
- You have difficulty understanding the words in the message. You have to work to understand the words.

3 = The delivery is **adequate** in meeting the requirements of the task. Examples are:

- The volume is not too low or too loud.
- The rate is not too fast or too slow. Pauses are not too long or at inappropriate spots.
- The pronunciation and enunciation are clear. The speaker exhibits few disfluencies, such as "ahs," "umhs," or "you knows."
- You are not distracted by problems in the delivery of the message.
- You do not have difficulty understanding the words in the message.

4 = The delivery is **superior** in meeting the requirements of the task. Examples are:

- The speaker uses delivery to emphasize and enhance the meaning of the message. The speaker delivers the message in a lively, enthusiastic fashion.
- The volume varies to add emphasis and interest.

SOURCE: © 1983, Massachusetts Department of Education. Reprinted with permission from *Development of the State Speaking Assessment Instrument: Reliability and Feasibility Study, 1983* and *Reliability and Feasibility Study, 1982,* State of Massachusetts, Department of Education, 350 Main Street, Malden, Massachusetts 02148.

- Rate varies and pauses are used to add emphasis and interest.
- Pronunciation and enunciation are very clear. The speaker exhibits very few disfluencies, such as "ahs," "umhs," or "you knows."

NOTE: In articulation you may be concerned with accent. However, articulation should be rated with respect to your ability to understand the message, not the social acceptability of the accent. One particular accent is not considered better than another. REMEMBER, in this component you are rating how the student speaks, not what the student says.

SOURCE: © 1983, Massachusetts Department of Education. Reprinted with permission from *Development of the State Speaking Assessment Instrument: Reliability and Feasibility Study, 1983* and *Reliability and Feasibility Study, 1982,* State of Massachusetts, Department of Education, 350 Main Street, Malden, Massachusetts 02148.

LANGUAGE

The language rating deals with the language which is used to convey the message. It is concerned with *grammar* and *choice of words*.

1 = The language is **inadequate** in meeting the requirements of the task.

■ The grammar and vocabulary are so poor that you cannot understand most of the message.

2 = The language is **minimal** in meeting the requirements of the task.

■ The speaker makes many grammatical mistakes.

■ The speaker uses very simplistic, bland language. The speaker uses a "restricted code," a style of communication characterized by simple grammatical structure and concrete vocabulary.

3 = The language is **adequate** in meeting the requirements of the task:

■ The speaker makes few grammatical mistakes.

■ The speaker uses language which is appropriate for the task, e.g., descriptive language when describing, clear and concise language when giving information and explaining, persuasive language when persuading. The speaker uses an "elaborate code," a style of communication characterized by complex grammatical structure and abstract vocabulary.

4 = The language is **superior** in meeting the requirements of the task.

■ The speaker makes very few grammatical mistakes.

■ The speaker uses language in highly effective ways to emphasize or enhance the meaning of the message. As appropriate to the task, the speaker uses a variety of language techniques such as vivid language, emotional language, humor, imagery, metaphor, and simile.

NOTE: In language you may be concerned with students who come from backgrounds where a foreign language or a nonstandard form of English is spoken. However, language should be rated with respect to your ability to understand the message, not the social acceptability of the communication style. If a speaker's use of incorrect or nonstandard English grammar interferes with your ability to understand the message, this fact should be reflected in your rating. REMEMBER, in this component you are rating how the student conveys the message through langauge, not what the student says.

SOURCE: © 1983, Massachusetts Department of Education. Reprinted with permission from *Development of the State Speaking Assessment Instrument: Reliability and Feasibility Study, 1983* and *Reliability and Feasibility Study, 1982*, State of Massachusetts, Department of Education, 350 Main Street, Malden, Massachusetts 02148.

ASSESSING "INTELLECTUAL QUALITY" OF STUDENT WORK

In order to understand the rubric, you need a little context. In the booklet from which these rubrics come, the authors' premise is that innovative teaching techniques (e.g., cooperative learning, group discussions, hands-on experiments, and videos) do not guarantee a change in the "intellectual quality" of what students are asked to do. For example, "a portfolio that shows a variety of student work over a semester might replace the final exam taken in one sitting, but the portfolio itself could be filled with tasks" devoted to remembering and listing isolated bits of information. Thus, the merit of any teaching technique should be judged by its ability to improve the "intellectual quality" of student performance.

Therefore, in the booklet, the authors attempt to define "intellectual quality," and then use this definition to develop three sets of rubrics: to judge the intellectual quality of the school work students are asked to perform, the intellectual quality of assessment tasks given to students, and the intellectual quality of student work that results from the tasks.

The rubrics were pilot-tested in mathematics and social studies. The booklet includes many examples in these subjects. But since the authors encourage application to any content area, the rubrics can serve to define delivery and performance standards across the curriculum and across teaching methods. The rubrics appear to be appropriate for about Grades 6 through 12.

There are three general standards for intellectual quality:

a. Construction of Knowledge—The mere reproduction of knowledge is not enough. Students need to know how to use that knowledge to make their own interpretations, evaluations, analyses, and syntheses. The authors don't expect students to perform like skilled adults, but they need to develop in that direction.

b. Disciplined Inquiry—This involves use of prior knowledge to strive for in-depth understanding rather than superficial awareness, and expressing one's own conclusions through elaborated communication. Again, the authors do not suggest that young students can be expected to make seminal contributions to the academic disciplines, but that they are capable of engaging in these forms of cognitive work when that work is adapted to students' levels of development.

c. Value Beyond School—Authentic achievements have meaning or value apart from documenting the competence of the learner. Adults use their information and skills to accomplish real tasks. We should help students to do this, too.

These three standards are applied in different ways to the three sets of rubrics in the booklet. Below, we present how the authors use these three standards to develop rubrics for the "intellectual quality" of student work. This is reproduced exactly from pp. 94-100 of the booklet.

SOURCE: © 1995, University of Wisconsin, Madison. From Newmann, F., Secade, W., & Wehlager, G. *A Guide to Authentic Instruction and Assessment.* Used with permission.

PART III: STUDENT PERFORMANCE

Overview and General Rules

Parallel, but somewhat differently worded, standards are presented for student performance in mathematics and social studies. The three standards reflect two of the general standards for authentic achievement as follows:

Construction of Knowledge: Analysis
Disciplined Inquiry: Disciplinary Concepts; Elaborated Written Communication

A. Scores should be based only on evidence in the student's performance relevant to the criteria. Matters such as whether the student followed directions, neatness, correct spelling, and so forth should not be considered unless they are relevant to the criteria.

B. Scores may be limited by tasks which fail to demand analysis, disciplinary conceptual understanding, or elaborated written communication, but the scores must be based only upon the work shown.

C. Scores should take into account what students can reasonably be expected to do at the grade level. However, scores should still be assigned only according to "absolute" criteria in the standards, not relative to other papers that have been previously scored.

D. When it is difficult to decide between two scores (e.g., a 2 or a 3), give the higher score only when a persuasive case can be made that the paper meets minimal criteria for the higher score. If the specific wording of the criteria are not helpful in making this judgment, base the score on the general intent or spirit of the standard described in the introductory paragraphs of the standard.

Mathematics

Mathematics Standard 1: Analysis

Student performance demonstrates thinking with mathematical content by organizing, synthesizing, interpreting, hypothesizing, describing patterns, making models or simulations, constructing mathematical arguments, or inventing procedures.

This standard is intended to measure the extent to which the student demonstrates higher order thinking (i.e., thinking that goes beyond mechanically recording or reporting facts, rules, and definitions or mechanically applying algorithms.

SOURCE: © 1995, University of Wisconsin, Madison. From Newmann, F., Secade, W., & Wehlager, G. *A Guide to Authentic Instruction and Assessment.* Used with permission.

The term "mathematical" analysis calls attention to the fact that the content or focus of the thinking should be mathematics. If analysis occurs about other subject areas, without a connection to mathematics, the performance would still score a 1 on this standard.

There are two guiding questions here: First, has the student demonstrated mathematical analysis? To answer this, consider whether the student has organized, interpreted, synthesized, hypothesized, invented, and so forth, or whether the student has only recorded, reported, or mechanically applied rules, definitions, or algorithms. If work is not shown, correct answers can be taken as an indication of analysis if it is clear that the question would require analysis to be answered correctly. Second, how often has the student demonstrated mathematical analysis?

4 = Mathematical analysis was used throughout the student's work.

3 = Mathematical analysis was used in 50% or more of the student's work.

2 = Mathematical analysis was used in less than 50% of the student's work.

1 = Mathematical analysis constituted no part of the student's work.

Example: If no work was shown and 3/4 of the questions were judged to require analysis to get the right answer, and the student did all of those correctly, she or he would score a 3 on this scale. On the other hand, if the student got them all wrong, he or she would get a 1. In short, the scorer should estimate the percent of the total task that the number of correctly answered analytic questions comprised.

Mathematics Standard 2: Disciplinary Concepts

Student performance demonstrates an understanding of important mathematical ideas that goes beyond application of algorithms by elaborating definitions, making connections to other mathematical concepts, or making connections to other disciplines.

This standard is intended to measure the extent to which the student demonstrates use and understanding of mathematical concepts. Prior to scoring the student's work, the rater should identify what mathematical concepts, if any, a student must use and/or understand to succeed in the task. Low scores may be due to tasks which fail to call for understanding of mathematical concepts.

A guiding question for using this standard is "Does the student show understanding of the fundamental ideas relevant to the mathematics used in the task?" Correct use of algorithms does not necessarily indicate conceptual understanding of the material. Such understanding can be demonstrated, for instance, by elaborating upon the concept through definition, or by making connections between the core concept and other related ones.

SOURCE: © 1995, University of Wisconsin, Madison. From Newmann, F., Secade, W., & Wehlager, G. *A Guide to Authentic Instruction and Assessment.* Used with permission.

If work is not shown, correct answers can be taken as an indication of conceptual understanding, if it is clear that the task or question requires a conceptual understanding in order to be completed successfully.

Completion of the task is not necessary to score high.

4 = The student demonstrates an exemplary understanding of the mathematical concepts that are central to the task. Their application is appropriate, flawless, and elegant.

3 = There is substantial evidence that the student understands the mathematical concepts that are central to the task. The student applies these concepts to the task appropriately; however, there may be minor flaws in their application, or details may be missing.

2 = There is some evidence that the student understands the mathematical concepts that are central to the task. Where the student uses appropriate mathematical concepts, the application of those concepts is flawed or incomplete.

1 = There is little or no evidence that the student understands the mathematical concepts that are central to the task, or the mathematical concepts that are used are totally inappropriate to the task, or they are applied in inappropriate ways.

Mathematics Standard 3: Elaborated Written Communication

Student performance demonstrates a concise, logical, and well articulated explanation or argument that justifies the mathematical work.

Performance that meets this standard could include, or consist of, diagrams and drawings as well as prose. To score high on this standard, the student must communicate, in writing, an accurate, complete and convincing explanation or argument.

The score should not be based on the proportion of student work that contains explanation/argument but on the quality of mathematical communication, wherever it may occur in the work. We use the prefix "mathematical" to draw attention to the fact that the substantive content of what is written about must be related to mathematics.

4 = Mathematical explanations or arguments are eloquent, clear, complex, and complete. Mathematical communication is exemplary.

3 = Mathematical explanations or arguments are present. They are largely concise, clear, and well articulated; however, they may be slightly flawed or incomplete in minor ways.

SOURCE: © 1995, University of Wisconsin, Madison. From Newmann, F., Secade, W., & Wehlager, G. *A Guide to Authentic Instruction and Assessment.* Used with permission.

2 = Partial mathematical explanations or arguments are present. They are incomplete because they have not been finished, they omit a major part of an argument, or they contain several mathematical or logical errors. *Note:* Simply showing work on algebraic problems (regardless of whether the answer is right or wrong) constitutes a low level of explanation and should be scored a 2 if no other part of the student's work on the task shows a higher level of communication.

1 = Mathematical explanations or arguments are absent or, where present, they are seriously incomplete, totally inappropriate, and incorrect. This may be because the teacher's questions have left no room for argument or explanation (e.g., fill-in-the-blank and multiple-choice questions).

SOURCE: © 1995, University of Wisconsin, Madison. From Newmann, F., Secade, W., & Wehlager, G. *A Guide to Authentic Instruction and Assessment.* Used with permission.

Social Studies

Social Studies Standard 1: Analysis

Student performance demonstrates higher order thinking with social studies content by organizing, synthesizing, interpreting, evaluating, and hypothesizing to produce comparisons/contrasts, arguments, application of information to new contexts, and consideration of different ideas or points of view.

This standard is intended to measure the extent to which students demonstrate cognitive activity that goes beyond mechanically recording, reporting, or otherwise reproducing information. Analysis may include proposing generalizations and supporting them with evidence; articulating and testing different theories or points of view; synthesizing and categorizing by applying abstractions to more specific information (this could include comparing similarities and differences); considering implications and application of information in new contexts; raising broad questions that help to interpret more specific information; or interpreting the meaning of personal roles, ideas, or events. The essential question is whether students demonstrate construction of knowledge through thinking and the organization of information, versus reproduction of knowledge by restating what has been previously given to them.

The rhetorical form of students' statements might qualify as analysis (e.g., "The main reason for the American Revolution was taxation without representation"), but to score high on analysis, the student's work must appear to be reasonably original, not merely a restatement of some analysis that was given previously in a text or discussion. In assigning a 3 or 4, the rater should be reasonably confident that no significant portion of the response has been virtually copied from some other source (i.e., text or oral statements of others).

4 = Substantial evidence of analysis. Most of the student's work includes analysis. At least three statements indicate that the student has successfully generalized, interpreted, tested, or synthesized specific information.

3 = Moderate evidence of analysis. A central portion of the student's work includes analysis. At least two statements indicate that the student has successfully generalized, interpreted, tested, or synthesized specific information.

2 = Some evidence of analysis. A small, but not central, portion of the student's work includes analysis. At least one statement shows that the student has successfully generalized, interpreted, tested, or synthesized specific information.

1 = No evidence of analysis. Almost all statements consist of recording, or reporting specific information, without evidence of the student's organizing it or reflecting upon it; OR virtually all analysis offered is unsuccessful or in error.

SOURCE: © 1995, University of Wisconsin, Madison. From Newmann, F., Secade, W., & Wehlager, G. *A Guide to Authentic Instruction and Assessment.* Used with permission.

In scoring analysis, the proportion of work that illustrates analysis is more important than the actual number of statements indicating analysis.

Social Studies Standard 2: Disciplinary Concepts

Student performance demonstrates an understanding of ideas, concepts, theories, and principles from the social disciplines and civic life by using them to interpret and explain specific, concrete information or events.

This standard is intended to assess the extent to which students use important ideas of the social disciplines to make concrete information and events more meaningful. Substantive concepts (e.g., depression, social class, culture) are often grounded in disciplinary knowledge from history and the social sciences, but many important ideas in social studies (e.g., justice, freedom, citizenship) may have no exclusive origins or associations within a single discipline. The main issue is the extent to which the student has used substantive social ideas to organize, explain, interpret, summarize, and extend the meaning and significance of otherwise discrete pieces of information.

Social studies concepts may be used even though they may not be stated explicitly, and this may vary with student grade level. For example, an elementary student's discussion of conditions or oppressed groups might indicate use and understanding of the concept of equality without stating the specific word.

If the topic of the task is itself a substantive idea (e.g., revolution), students should get full credit for successful use of it. Give credit only for ideas that are used appropriately in the context of the assignment. No credit should be given for serious errors in application or interpretation. The phrase "social studies concepts" means a minimum of one social studies concept.

4 = The student has used social studies concepts to organize, explain, interpret, summarize, and extend the meaning and significance of otherwise discrete pieces of information. The use of the ideas illustrates exemplary understanding.

3 = The student has included social studies concepts to organize, explain, interpret, summarize, and extend the meaning and significance of otherwise discrete pieces of information. The use of the ideas is somewhat limited and/or shows some flaws in understanding.

2 = Social studies concepts are included, but their use is significantly limited and/or shows significant flaws in understanding.

1 = The work includes virtually no social studies concepts, or the use of any that are included shows almost no understanding.

SOURCE: © 1995, University of Wisconsin, Madison. From Newmann, F., Secade, W., & Wehlager, G. *A Guide to Authentic Instruction and Assessment.* Used with permission.

The score for social studies Disciplinary Concepts should be based on the quality of use of social studies concepts, not on the proportion of student work that reflects social studies concepts.

Social Studies Standard 3: Elaborated Written Communication

Student performance demonstrates an elaborated account that is clear, coherent, and provides richness in details, qualifications, and argument. The standard could be met by elaborated consideration of alternative points of view.

To use the criteria below, the scorer should identify specific points in the student work that are elaborated and should make a judgment about the coherence of the overall framework in which various points are communicated.

4 = Exceptional: The writer provides substantial and accurate elaboration for two or more important statements. The details, qualifications, and nuances are expressed within an overall coherent framework intended for the reader and relevant to the topic. The response is so rich as to be worthy of display as an outstanding example of writing in social studies.

3 = Elaborated: The writer provides some elaboration for two or three important statements or provides substantial elaboration for one important statement. In either case, the details, qualifications, and nuances are expressed within a coherent overall framework intended for the reader, relevant to the topic, and without major inaccuracies.

2 = Minimal: The writer provides reasonably accurate elaboration for at least one important statement.

1 = Unsatisfactory: The writer provides virtually no information or provides only disjointed details OR the writer provides discrete claims, broad generalizations, slogans, or conclusions, but none are elaborated.

When a task includes several parts, the score for elaboration should be based on the part(s) answered in prose.

SOURCE: © 1995, University of Wisconsin, Madison. From Newmann, F., Secade, W., & Wehlager, G. *A Guide to Authentic Instruction and Assessment*. Used with permission.

RUBRICS FOR INFORMATION-PROCESSING STANDARDS

A. Effectively interprets and synthesizes information.

4 Interprets the information gathered for a task in accurate and highly insightful ways. Provides a highly creative and unique synthesis of the information.

3 Accurately interprets information gathered for a task and concisely synthesizes it.

2 Makes significant errors in interpreting the information gathered for a task or synthesizes the information imprecisely or awkwardly.

1 Grossly misinterprets the information gathered for the task or fails to synthesize it.

B. Effectively uses a variety of information-gathering techniques and information resources.

4 Uses the important information-gathering techniques and information resources necessary to complete the task. Indentifies little-known information resources or uses unique information-gathering techniques.

3 Uses the important information-gathering techniques and information resources necessary to complete the task.

2 Fails to use some significant information-gathering techniques and information resources necessary to complete the task.

1 Fails to use the most important information-gathering techniques or the major information resources necessary to complete the task.

C. Accurately assesses the value of information.

4 Analyzes information in detail, accurately and insightfully determining whether it is credible and relevent to a specific task.

3 Accurately determines whether information is credible and relevant to a specific task.

2 Makes some significant errors in determining whether information is credible and relevant to a specific task.

1 Makes little or no attempt to determine whether information is credible and relevant to a specific task or totally misjudges the relevance and credibility of information.

SOURCE: © 1993. McREL. Used with permission.

D. Recognizes where and how projects would benefit from additional information.

4   Insightfully determines the types of information that will benefit a task and effectively seeks out that information.

3   Accurately assesses a task to identify areas requiring additional information for clarification or support and seeks out the needed information.

2   Does not accurately assess the information needs of the task or fails to seek out needed information.

1   Makes little or no attempt to assess whether a task would benefit from additional information.

Glossary

So, what's in a word? A lot of confusion if folks are using terminology differently. Therefore, we present the following glossary of definitions *for the terms we use in this book*. Remember that there is not 100% agreement on some of these definitions. Regardless of whether or not you like *our* definitions, it is important to establish common agreement among your colleagues on the meaning of the terms *you* use.

Analytical trait scoring—Scoring procedure in which performances are evaluated for selected traits, with each trait receiving a separate score. For example, a piece of writing may be evaluated according to organization, use of details, attention to audience, and language usage/mechanics. Trait scores may be weighted and/or totaled. (see *Holistic* and *Primary Trait Scoring*)

Anchor—Representative product or performance used to illustrate each point on a scoring scale. The top anchor is sometimes called the exemplar. (see *Criteria, Rubric,* and *Scoring guide*)

Assessment—Any systematic basis for making inferences about characteristics of people, usually based on various sources of evidence; the global process of synthesizing information about individuals in order to understand and describe them better.

Authentic—Refers to assessment tasks that elicit demonstrations of knowledge and skills in ways that they are applied in the "real world." An "authentic assessment" task is also engaging to students and reflects the best current thinking in instructional activities. Thus, teaching to the task is desirable. (see *Performance assessment* and *Task*)

Bias and distortion—Factors, unrelated to the skill being assessed, that interfere with a valid inference regarding a student's true ability. For example, too much reading on a mathematics test might result in a distorted vision of a student's mastery of mathematics content. (see *Reliability* and *Validity*)

Constructed response—Assessment questions that require a student to produce a response rather than selecting it from a list. For example, essays, reports, oral presentations, reading fluency, open-ended mathematics problems, and so forth.

Content standard—Goal statement identifying the knowledge, skills, and dispositions to be developed through instruction. (see *Target*)

Criteria—Guidelines, rules, or principles by which student responses, products, or performances are judged. (see *Criterion-referenced* and *Evaluation*)

Criterion-referenced—Approach for describing a student's performance according to established criteria (e.g., she typed 55 words per minute without errors). (see *Criteria* and *Norm-referenced*)

Dispositions—Refers to the affective dimensions of students in school (e.g., motivation to learn, attitude toward school, academic self-concept, flexibility, persistence, and locus of control). Some scoring guides are designed to assess dispositions. These provide specific, observable indicators of the disposition being assessed.

Evaluation—Judgment regarding the quality, value, or worth of assessment results (e.g., "The information we collected indicates that students are reading as well as we would like"). Evaluations are usually based on multiple sources of information. (see *Criteria*)

Generic (general) criteria—Criteria that can be used to score performance on a large number of related tasks (e.g., a mathematics rubric that can be used to score problem solving regardless of the specific content of the problem). (see *Task-specific criteria*)

Holistic scoring—Scoring procedure yielding a single score based upon an overall impression of a product or performance. (see *Analytical trait scoring* and *Primary trait scoring*)

Norm-referenced—Describing a student's performance by comparison to other, similar students (e.g., she typed better than 80% of her classmates). (see *Criterion-referenced*)

Performance assessment—Assessment activity that requires students to construct a response, create a product, or perform a demonstration. Since performance assessments generally do not yield a single correct answer or solution method, evaluations of student products or performances are based on judgments guided by criteria. (see *Assessment, Criteria,* and *Task*)

Performance list—Scoring guide consisting of designated criteria but without descriptive details. For example, a performance list for writing might contain six features: ideas, organization, voice, word choice, sentence fluency, and conventions. Unlike a rubric, a performance list merely provides a set of features without defining the terms or providing indicators of quality. (see *Anchor, Criteria, Rubric,* and *Scoring guide*)

Performance standard—An established level of achievement, quality of performance, or degree of proficiency. Performance standards specify how well students are expected to achieve or perform. (see *Anchor* and *Content standard*)

Primary trait scoring—Scoring procedure by which products or performances are evaluated by limiting attention to a single criterion or a few selected criteria. These criteria are based upon the trait or traits determined to be essential for a successful performance on a given task. For example, a note to a principal urging a change in a school rule might have persuasiveness as the primary trait. Scorers would attend only to that trait. (see *Analytical trait scoring* and *Holistic scoring*)

Reliability—Degree to which the results of an assessment are dependable and yield consistent results across raters (interrater reliability), over time (test-retest reliability), or across different versions of the same test (internal consistency or interform reliability). Technically, this is a statistical term that defines the extent to which errors of measurement are absent from an assessment instrument. (see *Bias and distortion* and *Validity*)

Rubric—Set of general criteria used to evaluate a student's performance in a given outcome area. Rubrics consist of a fixed measurement scale (e.g., 4-point) and a list of criteria that describe the characteristics of products or performances for each score point. Rubrics are frequently accompanied by examples (anchors) of products or performances to illustrate the various score points on the scale. (see *Anchor, Criteria, Performance list,* and *Scoring guide*)

Selected response—Assessment questions that ask students to select an answer from a provided list (e.g., multiple-choice, matching, and true-false).

Scoring guide—Generic term for a criterion-based tool used in judging performance. In this book, we are using scoring guide synonymously with criteria and rubric. (see *Criteria, Performance list,* and *Rubric*)

Standardized—Set of consistent procedures for constructing, administering, and scoring an assessment. The goal of standardization is to ensure that all students are assessed under uniform conditions so that interpretation of their performance is comparable and not influenced by differing conditions. Both norm-referenced and criterion-referenced assessments can be standardized.

Task—Assessment exercise involving students in producing a response, product or performance (e.g., solving a mathematics problem, conducting a laboratory in science, or writing a paper). Since tasks are associated with performance assessments, many are complex and open-ended, requiring responses to a challenging question or problem. However, there can be simple performance tasks, such as reading aloud to measure reading rate. Tasks don't have to be exclusively used as stand-alone activities that occur at the end of instruction; teachers can observe students working on tasks during the course of regular instruction in order to provide ongoing feedback. (see *Assessment* and *Test*)

Target (as in "learning target")—Statement of what we want students to know and be able to do. (see *Content standard*)

Task-specific criteria—Scoring guide or rubric that can only be used with a single exercise or task. Since the language is specific to a particular task (e.g., to get a "4" the response must have "accurate ranking of children on each event, citing Zabi as overall winner"), task-specific guides cannot be applied to any other task without modification. (see *Generic (general) criteria*)

Test—Set of questions or situations designed to permit an inference about what an examinee knows or can do in an area of interest. (see *Assessment, Performance assessment*, and *Task*)

Validity—Indication of how well an assessment measures what it was intended to measure (e.g., does a test of laboratory skills really assess laboratory skills, or does it assess ability to read and follow instructions?). Technically, validity indicates the degree of accuracy of predictions or inferences based on an assessment measure. (see *Bias and distortion* and *Reliability*)

References and Further Readings

Chapter 1

Stiggins, R. (2001). *Student-involved classroom assessment* (3rd ed.). New York: Merrill.

Chapter 2

Blum, R., & Arter, J. (Eds.). (1996). *A handbook for student performance assessment in an era of restructuring* (Section VI). (Available from ASCD, 1250 N. Pitt, Alexandria, VA 22314; telephone 800-933-2723)

Illinois State Board of Education. (1995). *Effective scoring rubrics—A guide to their development and use.* (Available from Illinois State Board of Education, 100 N. First Street, Springfield, IL 62777)

Perlman, C. (1998). *The CPS performance assessment idea book.* (Available from Chicago Public Schools, 1819 W. Pershing Road, Chicago, IL 60609)

Rogers, S., & Graham, S. (1998). *The high performance toolbox.* (Available from Peak Learning Systems, 6784 S. Olympus Drive, Evergreen, CO 90349)

Wiggins, G. (1998). *Educative assessment.* San Francisco: Jossey-Bass.

Chapter 3

Goldberg, Gail, Maryland Department of Education; telephone 410-767-0100.

Blum, R., & Arter, J. (Eds.). (1996). *A handbook for student performance assessment in an era of restructuring* (Section VI). Alexandria, VA: ASCD.

Illinois State Board of Education. (1995). *Effective scoring rubrics—A guide to their development and use.* Springfield: Author.

Perlman, C. (1994). *The CPS performance assessment idea book* (pp. 4–7, 9, 10–14). Chicago: Chicago Public Schools.

Taggart, G. L., Phifer, S. J., Nixon, J. A., & Wood, M. (Eds.) (1998). *Rubrics—A handbook for construction and use.* Lancaster, PA: Technomic.

Wiggins, G. (1998). *Educative assessment.* San Francisco: Jossey-Bass.

Chapter 5

Guskey, T. (Ed.). (1996). *ASCD year book 1996—Communicating student learning.* Alexandria, VA: Association for Supervision and Curriculum Development.

O'Connor, K. (1999). *How to grade for learning.* Arlington Heights, IL: Skylight.

Chapter 6

NWREL. (1999). *Seeing with new eyes* (Video). IOX; telephone 310-822-3225.

NWREL's Six-Trait web site: http://www.nwrel.org/eval/writing

Spandel, V. (2001). *Creating writers.* New York: Longman.

Spandel, V., & Culham, R. (1996). *Writing from the inside out* (Video). IOX; telephone 310-822-3275.

Spandel, V., & Culham, R. (1999). *Seeing with new eyes.* NWREL; telephone 503-275-9500.

Index

Absolute scale approach, 76

Analytical rubrics, 18-21
  Assessing "Intellectual Quality" of Student
    work, 97, 169-176
  ATI Group Discussion, 97, 157-160
  Central Kitsap Mathematics, 96
  Central Kitsap Mathematics Rubric,
    69-70, 101-107
  Illinois Mathematics, 96, 108-109
  Juneau Primary Reading Developmental
    Continuum, 71, 96, 112-117
  Maryland Language Usage, 29, 97
  Massachusetts Oral Presentation, 97
  NWREL Informational Reading, 96
  NWREL Mathematics, 96, 110-111
  NWREL Six-Trait + 1 rubric, 97, 130-143
  Oregon Reading, 96, 121-125
  strengths/weaknesses, 22-25
  trait-scoring systems for, 41-43
  value-neutral trait definitions, 43

Anchor, 179

Arguments/refutation, 129

Art work assessments, 6-7

*Assessing Outcomes: Performance Assess-
  ment Using the Dimensions of Learning
  Model,* 36

Assessment methods, 2-3
  authenticity of, 179
  constructed response, 3
  definition, 179
  evaluation of, 180
  selected response/short answer, 2.
    See also Metarubrics

Assessment Training Institute. *See* ATI
  Group Discussion

ATI Group Discussion rubric, 97,
  157-160

Bias/distortion, 179

Bulletin boards, 84

Business letter rubric, 58-60, 68

California Mathematics rubric, 29, 96,
  98-100

Central Kitsap Mathematics Rubric, 69-70,
  96, 101-107

Checklists, 5-6

Chicago Public Schools, 36

Clarity traits, 48-49, 60-66

Communication:
  California Mathematics rubric and,
    98-100
  Central Kitsap Mathematics Rubric and,
    106-107
  Illinois Mathematics rubric, 108-109
  NWREL Mathematics rubric, 110-111

Conceptual understanding, 161-162

Constructed responses, 2-3, 181

Content/coverage traits, 46-47, 53-60
  ATI Group Discussion rubric and, 157
  McREL Rubric for Information-Processing
    Standards, 177-178
  standard for, 181

*CPS Performance Assessment Idea Book,
  The,* 36

Creativity:
  California Mathematics rubric and, 98
  rubrics and, 61

Criterion-references, 181
Critical thinking:
    Oregon Reading rubric and, 121-125
    strategies for teaching writing traits, 84-93

Debate, 131. *See also* Oral communication
Delivery skills. *See* Oral communication
Developing writer stage, 147-153
Dispositions, 181
Distortion, 180

Emergent readers. *See* Reading rubrics
Emergent writer stage, 145-146
Essay tests, 3
Evaluation of rubric. *See* Metarubrics

General Conceptual Understanding Rubric,
    97, 161-162
Generic (general) rubrics, 24, 26-28, 181
Grading, 77-81
    rubric conversion to, 73-74, 78-80
    score points and, 31
Great Tasks and More!, 36
Group interaction:
    ATI Group Discussion rubric, 97, 157-160
    clarity trait of, 62
    rubric for, 9
    teaching strategy of writing traits by, 91-
        92. *See also* Oral communication

Holistic rubrics, 18-19, 21
    California Mathematics, 29, 96, 98-100
    General Conceptual Understanding, 97,
        161-162
    Maryland Language Usage, 29, 97, 126
    scoring of, 181
    strengths/weaknesses, 21-22, 24-25
    Wauwatosa Developmental Continuum,
        29, 97, 144-156

Illinois Mathematics rubric, 96, 108-109
*Improving Classroom Assessment: A Toolkit
    for Professional Developers*, 36
Independent writer stage, 154-156
Information processing, 64
Informative scoring guide, 128

Juneau Primary Reading Developmental
    Continuum, 71, 112-117

KIRIS Grade 12 Mathematics Rubric, 67-68

Language:
    ATI Group Discussion rubric and, 158
    Maryland Scoring Rubric for Language in
        Use, 97, 126
    Massachusetts Oral Presentation rubric,
        168
    oral presentation rubric and, 57
    teaching criteria, 84-86
    usability in rubrics and, 51
Letter grading. *See* Grading

Maryland Scoring Rubric for Language in
    Use, 29, 97, 126
Marzano, Robert, 36
Massachusetts Oral Presentation rubric, 97,
    163-168
    score points of, 29
Mathematics assessments:
    analytical rubric for, 19
    California Mathematics rubric, 96, 98-100
    Central Kitsap Mathematics Rubric, 69-
        70, 96, 101-107
    examples of attributes for, 39-40, 42
    Illinois Mathematics rubric, 96, 108-109
    NWREL Informational Reading rubric,
        118-120
    NWREL Mathematics rubric, 96, 110-111
    rubric evaluation and, 67-68
McREL Rubric for Library Research, 97
McTighe, Jay, 36
Metarubrics:
    clarity trait, 48-49, 60-66
    content/coverage trait, 46-47, 53-60
    practicality/usability trait, 49-50, 66-69
    technical quality trait, 50-53, 69-71
Multiple choice responses, 2
Musical instruments, 3

NAEP Primary Trait rubrics, 27, 97, 127-129
Narrative scoring guide, 128
National Assessment of Educational Prog-
    ress, 27, 97, 127-129

National Council of Supervisors of Mathematics, 36

Negativity:
  rubric evaluation and, 51
  in scaling, 38

Norm-referenced, 181

Northwest Regional Educational Laboratory (NWREL). *See NWREL entries*

NWREL Informational Reading rubric, 96, 118-120

NWREL Mathematics rubric, 96, 110-111

NWREL Six-Trait + 1 rubric (student version), 97, 132, 134, 136, 138, 140, 142

NWREL Six-Trait + 1 rubric (teacher version), 97, 130-131, 133, 135, 137, 139, 141, 143

Objective test items. *See* Selected response/ short answers

On-Demand Speaking Rubric, 97, 163-164

Oral communication:
  assessment of, 2
  clarity trait of, 63-64
  Massachusetts Oral Presentation rubric, 97, 163-168
  On-Demand Speaking Rubric, 97, 163-164
  rubric evaluation and, 54, 56-58. *See also* Communication

Oregon Reading rubric, 96, 121-125

Organizational skills:
  constructed response assessments and, 3
  Massachusetts Oral Presentation rubric, 163

Peer-assessment, 83-93. *See also* Students

Performance criteria:
  benefits for students, 12-14, 16
  benefits for teachers, 16
  checklists/performance lists and, 5-8
  consistency in scoring through, 8-10
  definition, 3-4
  definitions, 181
  elucidating, 83
  grading, 77-81
  how to identify, 33-36
  importance of, 11, 14
  improved instruction through, 10-12
  need for, 2-3
  for parents, 15

setting standards, 74-77
  social studies, 97, 169-170, 174-176
  and standards-based education, 15-16, 182

Performance lists, 6-8, 181-182

Persuasive scoring guide, 129

Physical skills:
  analytical rubrics and, 23
  assessment lists for, 5
  assessment of, 2
  task-specific rubrics and, 29

Pickering, Debra, 36

Practicality/usability traits, 49-50, 66-69

Prewriter stage, 144

Primary trait scoring, 182

Problem solving:
  Central Kitsap Mathematics Rubric and, 104-105
  rubric evaluation and, 63

Reading rate:
  assessment of, 2
  performance criteria for, 4

Reading rubrics:
  Juneau Primary Reading Developmental Continuum, 71, 112-117
  NWREL Informational Reading, 96
  NWREL Informational Reading rubric, 118-120
  Oregon Reading rubric, 96, 121-125

Reasoning, 158

Regional Educational Laboratories, 36

Relative scale approach, 76-77

Reliability, 182

Research, 64

Rubrics:
  analytical rubrics, 18-21
  ATI Group Discussion, 97, 157-160
  California Mathematics, 96, 98-100
  Central Kitsap Mathematics, 96, 102-107
  conversion to grading, 73-74, 78-80
  creativity and, 61
  definition, 8, 182
  evaluating quality of. *See* Metarubrics
  examples of developmental attributes, 39-40
  generic, 24, 26-28
  holistic rubrics, 18-19, 21-22
  identification of performance criteria for, 33-36
  Illinois Mathematics, 96, 108-109

Juneau Primary Reading Developmental
    Continuum, 112-117
length of, 66
Maryland Scoring Rubric for Language in
    Use, 97, 126
Massachusetts Oral Presentation, 97
McREL Rubric for Library Research, 97
NAEP Primary Trait, 127-129
number of score points for, 29-31
NWREL Informational Reading, 96, 118-120
NWREL Mathematics, 96, 110-111
NWREL Six-Trait + 1 rubric, 97, 130-143
on-demand speaking, 97, 163-164
Oregon Reading, 96, 121-125
primary trait, 21
science, 179
sources for, 36
task-specific, 24, 25
Thinking Skills in Mathematics
    (U of Wis.), 97
Thinking Skills in Social Studies
    (U of Wis.), 97
Wauwatosa Developmental Continuum in
    Writing, 97, 144-156. *See also* Analytical
    rubrics; Holistic rubrics; Six-Trait Writ-
    ing Rubric

Scales of rubrics, 29-31, 75-77
Scoring consistency, 8-10
    choosing method for, 29-31
    informative scoring guide, 128
    Maryland Scoring Rubric for Language in
        Use, 97, 126
    narrative scoring guide, 127
    persuasive scoring guide, 129
    task-specific rubrics and, 28-29
Scoring guide, 182
Selected response/short answers, 2, 182
Self-assessment, 83
    Central Kitsap Mathematics Rubric and,
        102-107
Self-reflection, 39-40, 42
Short answers. *See* Selected response/short
    answers
Silverdale, Washington. *See* Central Kitsap
    Mathematics Rubric
Six-Trait Model:
    clarity trait of, 64-65
    content/coverage trait of, 60
    technical quality trait of, 70
    usability trait of, 68-69

Six-Trait Writing rubric, 20, 29, 31. *See also*
    the NWREL entries
Social studies rubric, 97
Speaking skills. *See* Group interaction; Oral
    communication
Standards-based education, 15-16
Students:
    analytical rubrics and, 22
    benefits of performance criteria for, 12-14
    and generic rubrics, 27
    identification of performance criteria
        via, 34
    identification of trait definitions via, 43
    performance criteria awareness for, 83
    performance criteria made public for, 15
    rubric development and, 36-40
Subjectiveness, 2

Task-specific rubrics, 24, 26, 28-29
    definitions, 182-183
Teachers:
    analytical rubrics and, 22
    benefits of performance criteria for, 8-12
    confidence of, 10
    and generic rubrics, 26-28
    performance criteria made public for, 15
    sample student work and, 36-38, 43
    strategies for teaching writing traits, 84-
        93, 85-86
    variance of grading and, 80
Teaching. *See* Instruction
Technical quality traits, 50-53, 69-71
Thinking Skills in Social Studies and Mathe-
    matics rubric, 97
Traits, 41-43. *See also* Analytical rubrics
True-false responses, 2

Usability traits. *See* Practicality/usability
    traits

Validity, 183

Wauwatosa Developmental Continuum in
    Writing, 29, 97, 144-156
Writing:
    assessment lists for, 5
    assessment of, 2
    effect of process of assessing on, 10

essay tests, 3
informative scoring guide, 130
NAEP Primary Trait rubrics, 129-131
narrative scoring guide, 129
NWREL Six-Trait + 1 rubric (student version), 97, 132, 134, 136, 138, 140, 142
NWREL Six-Trait + 1 rubric (teacher version), 97, 130-131, 133, 135, 137, 139, 141, 143
persuasive scoring guide, 129
teaching strategy of focused revision, 88, 90-91
teaching strategy of languages, 85-88, 90-93
teaching strategy of model revision, 91-92
teaching strategy of reading/scoring, 88, 90-91
teaching strategy of using language of traits, 92-93
Writing assessments:
analytical rubric for, 20
analytical rubrics and, 23
business letter rubric, 58-60, 68
examples of attributes for, 39-40, 42
rubric evaluation and, 54-55
Wauwatosa Developmental Continuum in Writing, 97, 144-156
Writing rubrics:
Maryland Scoring Rubric for Language in Use, 97, 126

CORWIN
PRESS

The Corwin Press logo—a raven striding across an open book—represents the happy union of courage and learning. We are a professional-level publisher of books and journals for K–12 educators, and we are committed to creating and providing resources that embody these qualities. Corwin's motto is "Success for All Learners."